marketing

Date Due			

LIBRARY

brilliant

marketing plans

What to know and do to make a successful plan

Ian Linton

Prentice Hall
is an imprint of

Harlow, England • London • New York • Boston • San Francisco • Toronto • Sydney • Singapore • Hong Kong
Tokyo • Seoul • Taipei • New Delhi • Cape Town • Madrid • Mexico City • Amsterdam • Munich • Paris • Milan

PEARSON EDUCATION LIMITED

Edinburgh Gate
Harlow CM20 2JE
Tel: +44 (0)1279 623623
Fax: +44 (0)1279 431059
Website: www.pearsoned.co.uk

First published in Great Britain 2011

© Pearson Education Limited 2011

The right of Ian Linton to be identified as author of this work has been asserted
by him in accordance with the Copyright, Designs and Patents Act 1988.

Pearson Education is not responsible for the content of third-party internet sites.

ISBN: 978-0-273-75629-3

British Library Cataloguing-in-Publication Data
A catalogue record for this book is available from the British Library

Library of Congress Cataloging in Publication Data
A catalog record for this book is available from the Library of Congress

10 9 8 7 6 5 4 3 2 1
15 14 13 12 11

Typeset in Plantin 10pt by 30
Printed and bound in Great Britain by Henry Ling Ltd, at the Dorset Press,
Dorchester, Dorset

Contents

About the author

Ian Linton, a graduate of the University of Bristol, is a professional writer and marketing consultant, specialising in business-to-business communications and management books. He has more than thirty years' experience in the business and has handled a wide range of marketing and communications programmes for international clients such as AT&T, Barclays Bank, BP Chemicals, Cisco, Dell, Ernst & Young, Ford, IBM, KPMG, Office of the Deputy Prime Minister, Shell, Siemens and Vauxhall. He is the author of more than twenty business books in the fields of marketing and customer service and has written a number of case studies for the Chartered Institute of Marketing.

Introduction: What makes a brilliant marketing plan?

Marketing success doesn't always come through an orthodox approach – brilliant marketing plans sometimes break the rules. That's because marketing planning is about winning – taking share from competitors or strengthening a vulnerable position against attack.

First, identify the problems and opportunities, then focus on strengthening your position. But don't overlook overall objectives; brilliant marketing plans integrated with corporate strategy deliver brilliant results.

So where do you start? A lot of very good books on marketing planning describe the formal process of planning. That's great if you want to get to grips with the basics. The problem is that marketing departments are under pressure to be more accountable and deliver measurable results that demonstrate an effective return on investment. It's time for action, not theory.

A brilliant planning toolkit

That's why this book focuses on outcomes, not processes. You'll find it's a practical toolkit to help you develop effective marketing plans quickly. The book provides a practical, project-based approach that enables you to put specific programmes into action quickly and effectively, without having to read an entire book.

Find out why it's important to add value to your products with services, open a new distribution channel or increase key account business. Learn how improving the customer experience or building market understanding of innovative products can transform market performance. These are the challenges that marketing teams face every day – get them right and you've got a marketing programme that demonstrates your importance to the business.

You'll find that each plan in the book is self-contained. That helps to reduce the time, effort and cost of creating marketing plans that deliver measurable results and improve competitive performance. However, individual marketing plans will be related to overall strategic objectives. That means you can create integrated marketing plans rather than a series of ad hoc solutions.

Each chapter includes a marketing plan in brief that shows how the projects relate to a conventional marketing plan structure. You can use that to build a more detailed plan for your own company by adding relevant information under the following headings:

Current situation

- Strengths.
- Weaknesses.
- Threats.
- Opportunities.

Market requirements

- What the market expects or requires from your company.

Objectives

- Your objectives for the project.

Strategy

- How you will deliver the project to meet your objectives.

Financial requirements

- The investment or funding you will require to complete the project.

Communications

- What you need to communicate to internal and external audiences.

Metrics

- How you will measure the success of the project.

What's your problem?

You'll find that the range of plans in this book covers challenges faced by marketing professionals and business owners in consumer and business-to-business sectors. Here's a brief outline of what you can deliver.

Products

Here we focus on plans for improving product performance. You'll find out how to develop a stream of new or improved products by adopting a platform strategy, learn how to ensure the success of that critical new product launch or add value to your product range by introducing customer services.

Market development

How can you improve your chances of success in the market? Educating the market will ensure that customers understand the benefits of your new product. You may need to reposition your company if customers have a poor perception of your products or your business. With customer preferences changing, opening a new distribution channel or communicating through new media will improve your chances of successful customer engagement.

Sales channels

The performance of your direct and indirect sales channels can have a major impact on the success of your marketing strategy. See why the sales force could benefit from a greater focus on customer relationships and how they can reduce the sales cycle to close more deals. Learn why companies are investing in key management and partnership with customers as a way of retaining major customers and controlling competitors. Find out how you can develop more business through your distribution channels.

Customers

The quality of customer experience has a direct impact on customer satisfaction and loyalty. Find out how to improve that experience and add value as a way of strengthening customer relationships.

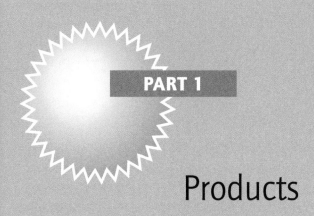

PART 1

Products

CHAPTER 1

Speed up product development

Product development is critical to your company's continuing success. Adopting a product platform strategy enables you to develop a stream of new or improved products based on a common design or platform. This approach speeds up the development process, reduces costs and lowers risk.

Product development and marketing strategy

Product development can help to meet many different aspects of your marketing strategy. These are some examples:

- Increase sales to existing customers.
- Take the company into new market sectors.
- Open new revenue streams.
- Position the company in different ways.
- Counter competitive activity.

Develop a product platform strategy

What is your strategy for developing new products? Do you have to develop different products for individual market sectors or key customers? Is your product range well balanced with new and mature products, or do you have too many old, declining products? A product platform strategy can help you to accelerate the product development process and respond rapidly to new market opportunities.

You can produce different versions of a core product for individual markets and customer segments by managing product designs using a platform strategy. The platform strategy reduces research and development effort and enables streams of products to be launched on the underlying platform. This approach also helps to control development and manufacturing costs when compared with producing a new version for each market.

If you have different product managers for different product groups or market sectors, they must take account of a platform strategy when they are planning new products or enhancements to existing products.

Create a roadmap

A product roadmap sets out your company's future direction for product development. The roadmap may be based on a platform strategy, developing future products on a common platform. Alternatively, the roadmap may set out proposals for new products that take advantage of emerging technologies or new, advanced materials. The roadmap gives product managers and other parties involved in product development a set of guidelines that coordinates their individual activities.

Follow a market-driven strategy

Your company's marketing strategy sets the requirements for product strategy by translating customer needs and challenges into product specifications. In some cases, marketing strategy might identify a need to improve existing products to meet competitive challenges or declining customer satisfaction levels. Marketing strategy might also require new products to meet changing customer needs or new market opportunities. Your platform strategy must take account of market strategies as it evolves.

Follow the product life cycle

Any product development decisions must also take account of the product life cycle – the stages a product goes through from initial launch through rapid sales growth to a point where sales decline. The four stages are introduction, growth, maturity and decline. Companies invest different levels of marketing or product development funding at each stage to maintain profitability. Product managers may decide to develop new features during a product's growth and maturity stages. However, investing in a product with declining sales is a waste of resources. The emphasis must now be on developing a new product.

Set standards

A product platform strategy enables you to establish standards and processes that other parties can work to when they collaborate with you. In the computer industry, for example, software companies provide independent developers with code and other forms of support so that they can develop additional new products that are compatible with the underlying platform. In the automotive industry, many major components are common to different car models. These platform products help manufacturers to control costs and take advantage of new technologies without major investment.

Research new products

Look for new products that meet customer needs. Innovation for its own sake does not guarantee success. Use market research to identify the strongest trends in customer needs. Check the websites of patent licensing agents. They list companies looking for inventions in different sectors and that information can highlight gaps in the market.

> innovation for its own sake does not guarantee success

Encourage innovation inside your company by setting up facilities on an intranet for employees to post suggestions. Set up a formal product development programme to identify ideas that represent strong market opportunities.

brilliant example

Michael Cusumano's book *Microsoft Secrets* (Simon and Schuster, 1995) describes the culture and processes that enabled Microsoft to bring so many innovations to market. According to the author, the key elements in the company's success include:

- Finding smart people.
- Organising small teams of overlapping specialists.
- Pioneering mass markets.
- Focusing creativity.
- Improving through continuous feedback.

Collaborate

Contact suppliers, business partners, research organisations and universities to source new ideas or to assess the commercial potential of projects that they are working on. License existing products or technologies from other organisations to expand your product range. Rebrand the products or offer them to consumers as own-label products.

Evaluate any innovation or suggestions to see if they provide a unique solution to a real problem. Compare the proposal to existing products and assess whether the differential would create a product that could generate revenue and profit.

Pharmaceutical research firm Biofocus finds that location on the Cambridge/Essex border is important to the success of its collaborative product development programme. The company is close to Cambridge University and a cluster of potential partners, including pharmaceutical manufacturers, biotechnology companies, patient organisations and charities which focus on developing solutions for specific diseases.

Locate and work with product development specialists who have promising ideas but who don't have the resources or the funds to turn their ideas into commercial products. To bring a product to market may require design engineering, prototyping, production, marketing and customer service resources which your company can provide.

Deal with declining products

Failing, outdated products consume management time, sales and marketing costs and production resource, while making a reduced contribution to revenue and profit. To deal with the problem, you need to analyse the reasons for poor product performance, create and implement a product development plan, and decide what to do with the failing products. It may be possible to market the failing products in a different way to earn continuing revenue – reducing their price or selling them into new markets, for example.

Analyse failing products

Look at sales over a period of time; declining sales are a clear warning sign that demand is falling or a product is failing. Compare the sales performance of competitors' products in the same market. If the competitive product continues to sell well, the problem relates to the product, not the market. Review the latest products to enter the market; if they are using newer technology, existing products may face further decline.

Analyse the reasons for product failure. Customers' needs or tastes may be changing. New technologies may offer superior performance. Existing products may have design or quality problems. Ask customers for their views on the products or check reviews and forums to identify customers' concerns.

brilliant example

Sony Corporation was a pioneer of the video recorder with its Betamax system. However, other consumer electronics manufacturers decided to adopt the alternative VHS system which became the standard for home video recorders, leaving Sony out of the market. When DVD emerged as a consumer technology, Sony participated in the standards group that worked to create a common format for DVD, ensuring that its product would be part of the mainstream.

Upgrade products

Put together a development plan, incorporating the findings from the product analysis. Identify opportunities and priorities for improving or upgrading existing products. Consider how new materials, new technologies or design changes could improve the product. Identify and fix any quality problems that affect product performance.

Change market focus

Look for new opportunities for outdated products. Consider offering them as budget versions of the new or improved product. Software companies, for example, offer home and professional versions of the same application program. In many cases, the home version is simply a two- or three-year-old version of the latest program. Identify market sectors where price, not product performance, is the important factor.

Reduce or cut marketing costs and find lower-cost production facilities for the older products. Drop products that have no scope for improvement or alternative marketing. Offer the product rights to potential buyers. Inform customers of the change and offer them alternative products. Dispose of any remaining stock with a cut price sale to customers or distributors.

Build a balanced product portfolio

Maintain a balanced product range of new and existing products to reduce any risk to the business. An effective product mix provides a balance of new and mature products, high margin or high volume products. It should also include older products that create revenue without requiring any marketing resources. Your portfolio should contain a mix of products that meet and exceed the needs of your customers.

> your portfolio should contain a mix of products that meet and exceed the needs of your customers

Analyse product mix

Analyse your current product mix. Identify the products that provide good profit margins or achieve growing sales in markets important to your business. Look for products that have no real differentiation from competitors' offerings. Classify your products by how quickly they sell.

Lower price commodity products sell quickly but generate lower margins. Although higher price products provide better margins, they sell slowly and may not make a major contribution to profit.

Use the analysis to assess your existing strengths and weaknesses and identify opportunities for improving the product mix.

Plan future mix

Carry out customer research to identify areas for improvement. Ask customers for a wish list of product improvements. Monitor feedback on product review sites or customer forums to identify current weaknesses or customer concerns. Compare your product specifications with competitive offerings.

Put together a development plan to improve the product mix. Prioritise opportunities to increase sales, create differentiation, improve profit margins or fill gaps in the current mix. Decide whether to retain or dispose of products that offer no scope for improvement. Upgrade the specification of products that currently offer little differentiation from competing products. Concentrate on improving features and performance criteria that are important to customers.

Focus on margins

Identify products that provide high profit margins. Look for opportunities to increase sales of those products to new or existing customers. Check that sales costs do not increase – selling high margin products can consume high levels of sales force time. Consider increasing prices of products with lower margins. Ensure that the products offer customers greater value than lower priced competitive offerings.

Fill gaps in the mix

Fill gaps in the product mix by introducing new products. Develop the new products internally if you have the resources, or work with partners that can supply existing products from their own range or develop the products you need. Ensure that your sales force has the skills and knowledge to sell the new products.

brilliant timesaver

Use a version strategy

Create different versions of existing products to increase market coverage. Add or remove product features to offer budget, standard and premium versions of the same product. Computer software is an example of this strategy where the same basic product is available in versions for home users, business users and advanced users, for example. This strategy enables you to reach different market sectors without introducing new products.

Review older products

Review the performance of older products in your mix. If products are still generating sales, consider retaining them, but reduce or stop any sales and marketing activity to minimise costs. If sales are declining or very low, drop the product from the mix. Alternatively, offer it to another company that operates in niche market sectors where the product has sales potential.

Develop products for global markets

If your company operates in export markets, use product design to match products with local requirements. Companies who follow the 'one size fits all' rule will not succeed globally because tastes, standards, prices, legislation and cultural differences influence customer choice from country to country. Effective product design must reflect global market requirements. Global companies like Nokia, Braun and Nike know that success is based on a single brand, but with many product design variations.

Use a platform strategy

Companies that operate in global markets manage their product designs using the platform strategy described earlier in the chapter. That allows them to create a 'core product' with different versions for individual territories.

Research into individual country requirements translates the product platform into a market platform plan. Market research identifies customer segments and priorities and maps local product offerings against those requirements. The product design team can then prioritise requests for local variations in line with individual market potential.

Maintain quality

While variation is essential, the key is to design the same level of quality into every market version. This allows you to create a strong brand that will be recognised and accepted in all territories. Marketing teams can then use that global brand strength to improve the effectiveness of their local campaigns.

Collaborate globally

To ensure they meet local needs, many multinational companies are creating global product design teams with employees or business partners from different territories. Forty-four per cent of respondents to the Aberdeen Group's 2005 'Product Innovation Agenda' study indicated that they are assembling teams across geographies to pursue global design. The Group's *Enabling Product Innovation* report indicated that one-quarter of companies are already outsourcing some design processes.

Marketing plan in brief

Current situation

- Existing portfolio of old and established products.
- Strength of established products.
- Weakness of changing customer preferences.
- Threat from new products introduced by competitors.
- Opportunity to capture market share with new products.

Market requirements

- Customers looking for increased product performance.

Objectives

- Increase sales to existing customers.
- Take the company into new market sectors.
- Open new revenue streams.
- Position the company in different ways.
- Counter competitive activity.

Strategy

- Develop a platform strategy.
- Research new products.
- Manage old or failing products.
- Build a balanced product portfolio.
- Tailor products for global markets.

Financial requirements

- Investment in product development programme.

Communications

● Build dialogue with customers to obtain product feedback.

● Communicate importance of innovation internally.

Metrics

● Increase in sales, revenue or profit generated by the new product.

● Increase in sales to existing customers.

● Sales to new customers.

● Gains from competitive accounts.

● Time to market.

● Product profitability.

brilliant recap

● Develop a platform strategy to create a stream of new products based on the same core product.

● Carry out continuous research and collaboration to find new products.

● Improve or drop old or failing products.

● Maintain a balanced portfolio of old and new products.

● Use a platform strategy to develop products tailored for global markets.

CHAPTER 2

Launch a new product

Launching a new product represents a high risk for any company. Months or years of investment, research and development resources have gone into the product. When the launch date comes, it's payback time.

Product launch and marketing strategy

New products can help to meet many different aspects of your marketing strategy. These are some examples:

- Increase sales to existing customers.
- Take the company into new market sectors.
- Open new revenue streams.
- Position the company in different ways.
- Counter competitive activity.
- Support a long-term platform strategy.

Set your launch objectives

Increase sales to existing customers

Are your customers buying products from competitors that you could supply? How well do you understand your customers' changing needs? They could be moving into new markets or facing challenges that they cannot overcome using existing products. Keep monitoring those customer needs throughout the product development process.

Take the company into new market sectors

Are you operating in market sectors that are crowded with competitors? Is growth slow in those sectors? Can you identify other sectors that offer better revenue and growth opportunities? If other sectors look promising, can you develop new products that would give you a strong market position?

Open new revenue streams

Are sales of existing products declining so that you need to open new revenue streams? Will the new product replace an existing one, or will it provide an additional source of revenue? New products can take time to get established in the market, so it's important to balance income from both new and existing products.

Position the company in different ways

Is your company seen as a market leader with innovative products, or is it perceived as one of many commodity suppliers in the sector? Do customers and prospects feel that you can meet only a limited part of their product needs? New products that offer higher value or greater levels of performance than other market offerings can change the perception of your company and make it easier for you to sell.

Counter competitive activity

Are you facing strong competition at important accounts? Do competitors offer a wider range of products aligned to customer needs or products that offer superior performance to your own? New products can help you to win business from competitors and increase your control over key accounts.

Support a long-term platform strategy

Are you developing a platform strategy that enables you to launch a succession of new releases based on a common core product? Your new product plan should support that strategy by setting a benchmark for the platform or filling gaps in the existing platform. Chapter 1 describes how to develop a product platform strategy in detail.

Meet customer needs

How well does the new product relate to customer needs? Your marketing strategy sets the requirements for new product strategy by translating customer needs and challenges into product specifications.

Listen to the customer

A successful launch has its roots in the early stages of product development when you are researching customer needs. Great inventions or technical breakthroughs don't necessarily make successful products – customer-focused solutions provide a greater guarantee of success. Listen to the customer to identify their needs. These are some possible scenarios:

> customer-focused solutions provide a greater guarantee of success

- Your customer must develop new products quickly to retain and protect market share and your new products are critical to their own product development programme.

- Your customers have to reduce their cost base to compete effectively and your new products will help them to succeed.

- Your customers need to improve their levels of customer satisfaction and your new products will prove vital to their success.

Build those needs into the product and into the launch communications programme.

Get customer feedback

Customer feedback on existing products can provide a valuable starting point for new product development. Carry out customer surveys or monitor product review websites to identify concerns or requirements.

brilliant tip

Ask customers for a wish list of new product requirements. Questions could include:

● How can we improve the current product?

● What problems need to be overcome?

● What new features would they welcome?

● Do the plans represent an improvement?

● Would they make greater use of a product that included the features they have highlighted?

In your launch communications, emphasise the ways in which new products reflect those customer needs.

Collaborate with customers

Product development can be a joint initiative where you work closely with specific customers to develop products that meet their specific needs. This approach can be driven by a number of factors:

● Your customers have developed partnership sourcing to take advantage of your technology.

- Your customer has technical skills that complement your own and a joint project can produce more effective results.
- Your customer has technology that will prove valuable to your own product development programme and there is an opportunity for mutual benefit.
- You want to strengthen relationships with key customers by working in partnership on joint development projects.

Collaboration on this level can significantly reduce the risk in a new product launch since both parties will be committed to the success of the product.

Customise products for individual customers

Take the collaboration process a stage further by customising products for key customers.

brilliant example

When Dell first allowed customers to configure personal computers online in 1996, they revolutionised e-commerce – buyers were no longer limited to standard, pre-packaged solutions. Now, customers expect manufacturers to offer products customised to their needs.

Offer more than a product

You can gain a major competitive advantage by offering customers 'complete products'. By providing services such as installation, training, technical support and maintenance, you can help customers make better use of the product throughout their period of ownership. Training and installation help customers use more complicated products immediately. Support and maintenance ensure that they continue to have full use of the product. Providing a 'complete product' offers your customers added value and gives you a differentiator that competitors may not be able to match.

providing a 'complete
product' offers your
customers added value

Prime the market

Before the launch, you can prepare the ground by priming the market and building understanding and awareness of the new product and its benefits. This is particularly important for innovative or technically complex products where benefits may not be obvious.

↗ brilliant impact

Make product announcements

If you are planning a succession of new products or upgrades to existing products, announce them in advance. This is an established practice in the computer software industry where companies announce new products on specific dates several times each year. That gives customers and prospects the opportunity to plan changes to their own business that take advantage of the new product.

Set out product line strategy

Setting out your product line or platform strategy achieves a similar result to a product announcement. Customers are aware that a range of products will be available at certain dates in the future. As a result, they may decide to postpone purchasing decisions until a specific product is available, creating advance demand for your product launch and pre-empting the purchase of competitive products.

Educate customers

If you are launching an innovative or complex product, plan a programme of customer education to ensure that customers understand the potential benefits. Publish discussion papers describing the application and benefits of the new products. Invite customers to seminars or arrange briefings with individual customers to build their interest.

Involve industry analysts

Industry analysts comment on developments in specific market sectors or product categories. They also provide consultative advice to companies on developments that will affect their future strategy. Briefing analysts on your new product plans ensures that your company will be considered at a strategic level.

Plan a go-to-market strategy

How will you take the new product to market? Will you sell the product through your own sales force or will you use distributors to reach a wider market? Could you use alternative channels such as direct sales via a website, direct mail or telemarketing? Your go-to-market strategy determines the sales and marketing resources you will need to allocate to the launch.

Use a direct sales force

Use your direct sales force when the sale requires contact at different levels in the customer organisation. Ensure that the sales force has the skills and market knowledge to understand and present the new product. Consider supplementing your own sales force with a contract sales team to provide complete coverage over the critical launch period.

Increase reach with distributors

A distributor network can take your new product to a wider market. This would be a useful strategy if your product is aimed at a large number of small customers that your own sales force could not cover cost effectively. Distributors also provide local market knowledge that may be useful in building initial sales of the new product.

Go direct

If you don't have a sales force or distributor network to take on the launch sales tasks, consider direct methods. Use direct mail or online marketing tools such as email to raise customer awareness or sell the product directly. Appoint a telemarketing team to contact prospects and take orders. The direct approach is more suitable for lower value products that do not require demonstration or customer education.

Build internal commitment

brilliant tip

Building internal motivation and commitment is essential to launch success. That means communicating effectively with all customer-facing staff, providing them with comprehensive product and launch information, and operating an incentive programme to encourage and reward greater effort throughout the launch.

Launch internally

Ask a senior executive to brief customer-facing staff on the strategic importance of the launch and the role of employees in the success of the launch. Ensure that all members of the sales force, customer service staff and service personnel take part in the internal launch. Hold a launch event such as a conference and make regular announcements as the programme moves towards launch date.

Provide launch information

Provide the sales force and distributor sales teams with information to help them sell the product. Launch information should include:

- Detailed product information.
- Product pricing.
- Profile of the target market.
- Customer problems that the new product overcomes.
- Benefits to the customer.
- Timetable for the launch.
- Marketing and advertising support for the launch.
- Sales targets.
- Incentive programme details.
- Customer service and post-launch support.

Operate an incentive programme

Encourage sales teams to put in a greater effort to ensure the success of the launch. Operate an incentive programme that is structured by sales of the new products to different groups of customers and prospects. The highest rewards would be based on sales to key accounts, followed by sales to new accounts and, finally, sales to existing customers. The incentive programme can also be aligned to other marketing objectives such as increasing volume and revenue, or selling to new sectors.

Develop launch communications

Support the sales teams with powerful marketing communications. Launch communications should include:

- Advertising to announce the new product in relevant consumer or business publications.
- Press releases and editorial in relevant publications.
- Website content providing new product information.
- Email or direct mail to customers and prospects.
- Participation in any major exhibitions that coincide with the launch timetable.
- Customer events to introduce or demonstrate the new product.

Setting prices

Setting product prices can be one of the most challenging aspects of a new product launch. Pricing strategy must strike a balance between building high levels of initial sales through competitive pricing and maintaining margins that ensure a good return on the investment in new product development.

Take advantage of first-to-market pricing

If your product is the first of its type in the market and has no direct equivalent, you can adopt an aggressive pricing strategy without fear of undercutting by competitors. Provided your product meets clearly identified customer needs and offers strong benefits, set a premium price for the launch period. However, you may have to adjust prices if competitors catch up and introduce their own version of the product at lower prices.

Offer trial version pricing

One way to improve revenue at the launch is to offer trial versions of the new product at special introductory prices. This can increase revenue as well as overcoming any hesitation that prospects might have about buying the product. Customers can pay a lower price for the trial version and upgrade to a full version of the product when they are satisfied with performance.

Operate a differential pricing strategy

Offer different customer groups a range of prices or price packages for the same basic product. For example, you could offer 'first-class' or 'economy' prices. First-class customers receive extra value, such as faster delivery or complementary services, by paying a premium price. Economy customers pay a lower price but would get just the basic product, with no added value. This type of price segmentation can help you reach different markets without changing the specification or costs of your new product.

Ensure successful adoption

To ensure the success of the launch, ensure that there is a service infrastructure in place to help customers use the new product. Announce success stories to maintain the momentum of the launch.

Prepare the service infrastructure

Train the field service teams so that they are ready to provide installation and maintenance of the new product. Offer customers a portfolio of services to supplement their own support resources. Set up a helpdesk to handle customer queries and technical issues. Put a mechanism in place to deal with any product problems that come to light after launch.

Celebrate success

Publish case studies of successful customer installations to build confidence in the new product. Ask customers if they are willing to act as reference sites so that prospective buyers can approach them for information. Set up a forum where customers can discuss their experience with the product or provide feedback.

Marketing plan in brief

Current situation

- New product critical to company's success.
- Strength of customer base and sales channels.
- Weakness of existing product range.
- Threat of competitive offerings with superior performance to company's existing range.
- Opportunity to increase market share and enter new markets.

Market requirements

- Demonstration of commitment to new product development.
- Improved product performance.

Objectives

- Increase sales to existing customers.
- Take the company into new market sectors.
- Open new revenue streams.
- Position the company in different ways.
- Counter competitive activity.
- Support a long-term platform strategy.

Strategy

- Research customer needs.
- Prime the market with product announcements.
- Plan a go-to-market strategy.
- Build internal awareness and commitment to the launch.
- Operate launch programme.

Financial requirements

- Develop pricing plan.
- Establish launch budget.

Communications

- Internal communications to raise awareness of sales and customer service teams.
- Customer and prospect communications to announce new product.

Metrics

- Increase in sales, revenue or profit generated by the new product.
- Increase in sales to existing customers.
- Sales to new customers.
- Gains from competitive accounts.

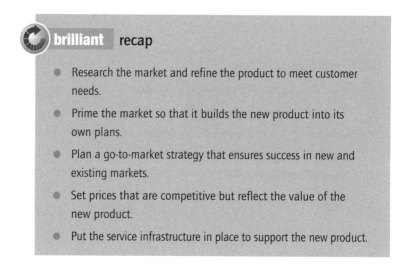

brilliant recap

● Research the market and refine the product to meet customer needs.

● Prime the market so that it builds the new product into its own plans.

● Plan a go-to-market strategy that ensures success in new and existing markets.

● Set prices that are competitive but reflect the value of the new product.

● Put the service infrastructure in place to support the new product.

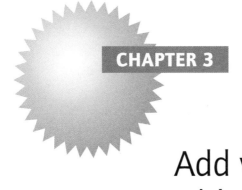

CHAPTER 3

Add value with service

Offering added-value services enables your company to strengthen relationships with customers by helping them to improve their business performance throughout a 'life cycle'. While high value professional services such as consultancy provide customers with important strategic benefits, customers may also need longer-term support to effectively implement recommendations and gain real business benefit. Services such as training, project management and facilities management have therefore become important elements in providing the client with a 'total business solution'.

Service solutions and marketing strategy

Developing service solutions can help to meet many different aspects of your marketing strategy. These are some examples:

- Strengthen relationships with existing customers.
- Open new revenue streams.

Identify service opportunities

Planning begins with research into customers' service needs. One of the most effective ways to identify service opportunities is to look at the problems customers face by analysing a series of business scenarios.

planning begins with research into customers' service needs

Some examples show how the process works:

- Your customers need to ensure that they have devised the right strategy to meet their business goals. They need objective advice and guidance to improve the quality of their own decision making. You can meet those requirements by offering consultancy services.

- Customers have identified certain activities that are crucial to their business success. They need help in defining the problems and planning the most appropriate course of action. Consultancy will also be relevant here.

- Your customers need to adapt quickly to changing market conditions or competitive threats, but they do not have the resources or skills to succeed. You can offer customers skilled staff and other resources on a project basis so that they can meet short- and long-term requirements.

- Customers need to develop new user and management skills so that they can get the best return from an investment. You can offer your customers training service.

---

brilliant example

Andersen Consulting introduced services such as facilities management and managed service to complement their traditional information technology consulting activities.

In the human resources sector, recruitment consultants Austin Knight decided to get more deeply involved with their clients' whole personnel strategy by introducing a range of internal marketing consultancy services to support change management in their clients' organisations. Technology marketing consultancy Wilson Miller offered their clients a resourcing service that provided high calibre marketing staff for medium- and short-term projects.

Assess customer needs

To take advantage of the service opportunity, your plan should cover the following stages:

1 Assess your customer's service needs.

2 Identify service opportunities at each stage of the customer life cycle.

3 Compare service requirements with the services you are already delivering.

4 Introduce the new services.

5 Use the service offering to build stronger relationships with your customers.

As an example, the need to improve competitiveness and reduce costs is driving many companies to investigate the potential of information technology strategies such as cloud computing. Implementing that kind of strategy can have far-reaching consequences, and vendors have an opportunity to offer their customers a wide range of integrated services, including strategy development, migration planning, hosting, change management, and training and support.

Analyse customer life cycles

Another way to identify service opportunities is to look at customers' life cycles – what type of support does a customer need at different stages of its life and how can your services help them achieve better business performance? The most important stages in the life cycle are described as:

1 Consult.

2 Design.

3 Implement.

4 Manage.

Consult: At this stage, the customer's executive team decide on their overall strategy for dealing with key business issues. This is the most important stage for influencing the shape of future policy, and your company should be involved at this stage, particularly if competitors are trying to influence senior decision makers.

Design: The customer has decided the overall strategy and is consulting with individual departments to design specific solutions or incorporate individual requirements into the service specification.

Implement: At this stage, the new service has been introduced and the customer concentrates on getting the service up and running as quickly as possible, with minimal disruption to day-to-day operations.

Manage: The manage stage is the equivalent of normal operation. The service has been used successfully and the customer's support task is to ensure it continues to be used effectively and delivers business benefits.

---

brilliant example

As an example, take the introduction of a new computerised accounting system in a small to medium-sized company. The company may be growing rapidly and have no real experience of computerised accounting. An accountancy practice can provide valuable support at each of the four life cycle stages.

Consult

- Helping the customer to plan an accounting system to meet current and future needs.

- Advising on the management and training implications of the new system.

Design

- Setting a detailed specification for the system.
- Advising the customer on suitable hardware, software and procedures.

Implement

- Providing initial guidance to client staff on using the new system.
- Recommending or providing training services.

Manage

- Reviewing the operation and benefits of the system.
- Advising on new software to meet changing operating requirements.

The life cycle concept can be applied to a number of business scenarios, particularly where customers are introducing new technology or new working practices. The important thing is that customers' needs change at each stage and their own support team may not have the skills or resources to handle all of these tasks cost effectively. By analysing a customer's life cycle your company can develop a range of services that will provide all the help and guidance that is needed, and will be able to maintain high levels of contact with the customer throughout the life cycle.

Develop service capability

Before you plan your service capability, consider customers' needs in order to identify the type of services you need to develop.

- Do your customers face any of the problems described in the business scenarios?
- How well do you understand the business issues faced by your customers?

- Is new legislation likely to impact on customers' business? How could your services help them to overcome potential problems?
- Can you identify the customer life cycle that is relevant to the services you provide?
- What stage of the life cycle are your customers currently in?
- Can you offer your customers services that would improve their business performance at current and future life cycle stages?

If this analysis shows that services are important to your customers, what sorts of services are required and what is their value? How can you deliver quality service cost effectively?

Identify revenue opportunities

Although a key role is to improve relationships with customers, services can also make an important contribution to revenue. One computer company, for example, found that customer services contributed around 25 per cent of turnover and nearly 50 per cent of profits, and it is significant that many manufacturing companies now recognise that an important part of their future is as a service company.

> many manufacturing companies now recognise that an important part of their future is as a service company

brilliant example

IBM transformed itself from a computer manufacturing company to a global services company because it recognised that one of its customers' most important requirements was to make the most of their investment in the products they had already bought. Companies that have traditionally provided their customer services free now have to set up changing structures and persuade their customers that the services represent value for money.

Assess service capability

Identify the services you plan to offer. Companies outsource services primarily to reduce costs or to utilise skills and resources that they do not have in-house. Do you have the skills and resources to offer those services at a cost that is lower than the internal cost? Customers will be concerned about outsourcing services, particularly if the services are critical to their business. The more strategic the service, the higher the risk to the company. You must be able to demonstrate the capability to deliver a reliable, quality service.

Demonstrate capability

Customers will check suppliers' credentials carefully before selecting a service provider. They will be looking for suppliers who are financially viable, with the resources to handle current outsourcing tasks and the capacity to meet any increased requirements in the future. Develop communications material to prove your capability. These are some of the key features that customers are looking for in a service offer:

- One contact point simplifies contact and service administration.
- Nationwide resources ensure that support is available wherever the customer is located.
- Direct contact with a technical specialist provides immediate response to problems or queries.
- Quality support to ISO 9000 gives independent reassurance that service standards are high.
- Support round the clock means that support is available when the customer needs it, minimising downtime.
- Complete support solutions provide support to meet all a customer's needs with consistent service standards.

- Service options give a choice of service levels which can be aligned to the customer's needs.
- Investment in support means long-term commitment to the customer.

Develop performance standards

Work with the service team to develop stringent service level agreements (SLAs) to ensure that your service meets customers' performance objectives. Establish key metrics and a process for measuring and reporting performance. Set up a process for regular customer reviews to monitor progress, and consider penalty clauses for underperformance.

Work with service partners

If services are important to your business, but you do not have the resources to deliver them yourself, consider working with service partners. Select a service partner using the same criteria that customers use to evaluate service providers. Impose strict quality standards and carry out a risk assessment to identify any potential weaknesses in the arrangement. The Homecall+ service, for example, utilises a network of approved contractors to provide home emergency repairs.

Market services

A life cycle marketing programme is a good basis for developing effective long-term relationships with your customers. The life cycle recognises that customers progress through different stages in their utilisation of a programme and this enables the company to identify opportunities to support the

> a life cycle marketing programme is a good basis for developing effective relationships with customers

customer. This in turn can help to build stronger business relationships and help you to develop a long-term strategy for delivering customer service.

To make the most effective use of the life cycle approach, you need to develop an understanding of your customers' business processes and get to know the skills and resources available. The life cycle provides an opportunity to take over complete services on the customer's behalf or to supplement their resources when they need help most.

An effective marketing strategy for services identifies your key service product and people strengths and creates a customer offer based on leadership in knowledge, skill and sector experience. The aim is to differentiate your company's services and demonstrate their strategic value to the customer.

Build a portfolio

Build a services portfolio that matches customers' needs throughout the life cycle of a product. For example, an organisation providing equipment services could offer consultancy, planning, design, installation, training, maintenance and upgrade services to the same customer. This creates a long-term revenue stream and strengthens the customer relationship. Fill any gaps in the portfolio by developing new services or working with qualified service partners.

Segment the market

Structure services to meet the needs of different market sectors. If you have specific industry experience or skills, you can structure your services by vertical market. The industry insight provides a differentiator that competitors may not be able to match. You can offer customers different levels of service, such as gold, silver or bronze. Customers can choose the level of service that meets their operational needs and budgets.

Develop customer service skills

Run ongoing training and development programmes for customer-facing staff. Provide access to knowledge bases and collaborative tools to enable staff to enhance skills and deliver a high quality service to customers. Consultants Deloitte operate a social networking site for employees that enables them to share knowledge and to access skills from any location in the firm's global network.

Demonstrate your service credibility

Use thought leadership tools such as conference speaking, articles and white papers to build credibility in the marketplace. Research indicates that a high proportion of decision makers used referrals and information gathered from sources such as articles, blogs and case studies to identify potential service providers.

Raise awareness

Make customers and prospects aware of the benefits of services to their business. Develop educational programmes to help customers identify how services can improve their business. Use financial tools to demonstrate the potential return on investment from services. Technology consultancy, for example, can help customers make informed decisions about their future technology investments. Maintenance services can help customers run their operations more efficiently with less risk of disruption.

Build stronger relationships

Develop knowledge-based relationships with customers. Capturing knowledge from employees and service delivery projects provides a basis for a portal that customers can use to get answers to simple service queries. The knowledge base improves customer convenience and helps to strengthen relationships.

Strengthen brands through service value

⁊ brilliant impact

Service products have a direct impact on the strength of a brand because they influence a customer's experience of the brand. Quality service improves customer perception of the brand; poor service has the opposite effect. One customer's poor experience can have a multiplying effect as customers share their experience through social media.

Improve service experience

Brand strength is determined by two main factors: customers' satisfaction with the product itself and their experience in acquiring or using the product. Service products create an interaction between the customer and the brand that must be managed carefully. If a customer chooses a brand and orders it by telephone, the quality of telephone response and call handling affects brand perception. If the customer signs a maintenance contract for the product and service delivery is poor, that experience also impacts the brand.

Create brand relationships

Service products create relationships between a brand and a customer. In consumer markets the service relationship might be simple, with the customer taking out a finance agreement and an extended maintenance warranty. In business-to-business markets longer-term service relationships are more common. Here, service products might include consultancy, installation, training, maintenance and upgrades. Each of those service relationships creates a customer experience and an opportunity to strengthen – or damage – the brand.

Maintain quality

the investment in service quality is as important as the investment in product quality

Services can reflect on the quality of a brand because they form part of the customer's experience of the brand. That means you must set and maintain quality standards for every service product and every point of customer contact. To build and strengthen a brand, the investment in service quality is as important as the investment in product quality.

Build value

Service products have a double impact on brands. Not only can they strengthen the intangible value of the brand by increasing and improving customer experience of the brand, but they can also increase the financial value of the brand by generating additional revenue streams. That makes service development and quality control a key element in brand management.

Marketing plan in brief

Current situation

- Company provides products, but customer sources service from third-party providers.
- Strength of existing customer relationships.
- Weakness of lack of service capability.
- Threat of third-party vendors or competitors gaining account control.
- Opportunity to increase account control and open new revenue stream.

Market requirements

- Customer has service and support requirements at different stages of their life cycle.

Objectives

- Strengthen relationships with existing customers.
- Open new revenue streams.

Strategy

- Identify service opportunities.
- Develop service capability.
- Market services.
- Brand services.

Financial requirements

- Develop pricing plan for services.
- Invest in services infrastructure.
- Allocate services marketing budget.

Communications

- Communicate service capability to customers.
- Demonstrate value of services.

Metrics

- Revenue from service offerings.
- Customer retention levels.
- Customer satisfaction levels.

brilliant recap

- Identify service opportunities using the customer life cycle.
- Develop a quality service capability.
- Market services to demonstrate their value to customers.
- Strengthen your brand through the value of quality services.

PART 2

Market development

CHAPTER 4

Educate the market

nnovative products can give your company a strong competitive advantage, but only if customers understand the potential benefits. Innovation for its own sake is unlikely to create a great market opportunity if the product does not meet customer needs.

Market education and marketing strategy

Market education can help to meet many different aspects of your marketing strategy. These are some examples:

- Increase sales to existing customers.
- Improve sales force productivity.
- Open new revenue streams.
- Position the company in different ways.
- Ensure the success of a product launch.

Research customer needs

Before you even consider a market education programme, take a step back. Carry out product and market research to ensure that you understand your customers' needs. Work with them to help them develop wish lists of features they are looking for in new products. In your research, ask questions to see if customers understand the full benefits of new features that you plan to introduce.

As product development progresses, conduct further customer research, showing concepts and analysing response to identify any issues in understanding. Use this research as the basis for a market education programme to build momentum and understanding before the launch.

▶ brilliant example

When BP Chemicals launched a range of high performance composites, they found that engineers and designers were not aware of the potential of the new material to solve long-standing design challenges. Through a designer's guide, which explained the applications and showed examples of successful products used in extreme conditions, they encouraged designers to think creatively and to look for different solutions to their problems.

The key to success for companies in this situation is to build trust and position themselves as advisers, rather than sales people.

Build understanding

thought leadership is a key element in building market understanding and influencing decision makers

Thought leadership is a key element in building market understanding and influencing decision makers. Articles in important publications, speaking appearances at industry events, well-produced customer magazines, white papers, podcasts and webcasts can all help to build understanding and preference for the company's products and services and position a company as a trusted expert.

Speak at conferences

Providing quality keynote speakers at a customer event not only forms an important part of the customer education process but also raises your company's profile. You can achieve the same results by getting on discussion panels or conference workshops. If you are participating in an external event, organisers publish dates for submission of conference papers, so make sure you are aware of those dates and provide suitable material. Again, focus on providing useful information. You are there to inform and educate, to provide a unique perspective. If your speaker is selected, promote their presentation in pre-event publicity and publish their papers in your post-event communications.

Arrange executive briefing meetings

Executive briefing meetings give you the opportunity to bring your customers up to date with new developments in your business or in your industry that might benefit them. For example, you might brief them on new technical developments or new legislation that is likely to impact on them. This type of meeting not only demonstrates your professionalism and builds thought leadership, it also helps to add value to the customer relationship. This is an important part of the process when the discussion of new products needs to move from technical to business decision makers.

brilliant example

Cisco Systems recognised that communications networks were not just transport systems for voice and data traffic, they were powerful business tools capable of transforming the way companies operated and collaborated with other organisations. To communicate that message and build understanding, they had to move the discussion from the IT department to the boardroom with a programme of executive education.

Provide useful information on your website

Your website should provide a source of useful information for customers, prospects and influencers. When you are introducing innovative products, your website can be a valuable source of information for decision makers and users who need more detailed information.

You should therefore include:

- Copies of white papers and case studies for downloading.
- Designers' guides.
- Bulletins on research you are carrying out.
- Copies of seminar or conference papers delivered by your own speakers.
- Copies of published articles or news items that discuss the new product.
- Details of events where your company is participating.
- Blogs commenting on industry issues that your product is addressing.

Make the most of white papers

White papers and case studies help to build understanding and awareness. They are useful resources that demonstrate you understand and care about the problems that your customers are trying to solve. Your white paper should review problems or needs faced by the reader, rather than describe a product or service offered by your company.

your white paper should review problems or needs faced by the reader

White papers should be clearly written and illustrated and may need the skills of a writer or editor, as well as a technical specialist. Making high value technical information available through white papers can strengthen customer relationships.

brilliant tip

White papers are an important tool for communicating with technical decision makers. They are widely used by companies marketing business-to-business and technology products.

White papers help people make decisions. In the IT sector, industry research indicates that around 70 per cent of IT professionals in the United States rely on white papers to make purchasing decisions. They are particularly valuable in the early stages of purchase when decision makers are gathering information.

Understand user needs

In business, white papers provide information that enables readers to evaluate products, services or technologies. In the IT sector for example, choosing the right technology has become critical to business success. Product evaluation has therefore become more intense, particularly on large-scale projects. Preparing a technical – and financial – justification is an extremely rigorous process. The detailed information available in white papers meets part of that research process, providing documentation that can guide and support decision making.

White papers fall into a number of different categories, including:

- Technology guides – explaining a product's technology, why the technology is important to potential customers, and how it's different from and better than similar technologies.
- Position papers – explaining a trend, or technology.
- Business guides – explaining the business and financial benefits of a product or service.
- Competitive reviews – evaluating a company's products and comparing them with similar competitive offerings.
- Product guides – providing a detailed description and explanation of a product's features and functionality.

● Application guides – describing the application of a product or technology in a particular industry.

Inform readers, don't sell

A white paper should be a piece of information, not a sales document. A good test is to avoid mentioning your company or your product in the first half of the white paper. If prospects feel that you are trying to sell, rather than inform, the white paper becomes less valuable, and is treated as a marketing message. Your white paper should therefore review problems or needs faced by the reader, rather than describe a product or service offered by your company. You can also maintain the educational value of the paper by talking about your product in generic terms, rather than by brand name – 'products with these features help to overcome these issues', for example. If you take this approach, you can mention your product name at the end of the document in a 'sign-off' which is separated from the main text of the document.

Write at the appropriate technical level

brilliant dos and don'ts

Although white papers are regarded primarily as a medium for technical readers, it's important to write at the correct technical level. You should not assume that your readers will be familiar with technology, particularly if it is new technology. You should therefore avoid jargon and use charts, diagrams or other forms of visual treatment to clarify complex ideas. Wherever possible, use industry-standard terminology, rather than your company's marketing language. A glossary of terms would be useful for complex products or services.

You should remember that white papers may also be read by non-technical readers. If communicating with business decision makers is one of your important objectives, you must ensure that the content is understandable to a non-specialist audience. Some companies produce several versions of the same paper, with a description on the front cover such as 'this publication is intended for technical readers' or 'this publication is intended for executive decisions makers'.

Make it easy to access your white paper

Because of their important role in purchasing decisions, white papers are now widely available as downloads on suppliers' websites. The internet has become a key medium for product research and white papers are an integral part of that process. This enables you to distribute information to prospects in a very accessible and cost-effective way. You should make it easy for visitors to find your white papers:

- Create a library listing all the white papers available.
- Place links to white papers on pages where you describe relevant products or industry solutions.
- Place a list of white papers on your press information page.

You can also distribute white papers through companies who specialise in syndicating white papers for a particular industry. These companies offer readers a wide range of material from different suppliers so that readers can compare different offerings.

Marketing plan in brief

Current situation

- The company manufactures innovative products.
- Strength of product range and corporate reputation.
- Weakness of market understanding of new product benefits.
- Threat of slow market adoption of new products.
- Opportunity to raise awareness and increase market penetration.

Market requirements

- Education and information on product applications and benefits.

Objectives

- Increase sales to existing customers.
- Improve sales force productivity.
- Open new revenue streams.
- Position the company in different ways.
- Ensure the success of a product launch.

Strategy

- Research customer awareness and understanding.
- Use thought leadership and education to improve understanding.
- Publish white papers to communicate innovation.

Financial requirements

- Establish budget for programme communications.

Communications

- Thought leadership and educational content.

Metrics

- Sales to existing customers.
- Changes in sales force productivity.
- Revenue from services.
- Changes in perception of the company.

brilliant recap

- Research customers' understanding and awareness of your product's benefits.
- Develop a programme of market education to improve understanding.
- Raise the discussion to board level to highlight strategic importance of the product.
- Make the most of thought leadership tools such as white papers.

CHAPTER 5

Reposition a company

Positioning is the perception customers or the market has of a product or company. It is an important way to differentiate a company and support long-term sales and profit objectives. It should be based on factors that are relevant to customers and hard for competitors to match.

Positioning and marketing strategy

Positioning can help to meet many different aspects of your marketing strategy. These are some examples:

- Increase sales to existing customers.
- Take the company into new market sectors.
- Open new revenue streams.
- Counter competitive activity.
- Support a long-term business development strategy.

Assess your positioning

How do customers perceive your company? Do they understand your direction, mission and values? Are they aware of your strengths and achievements? How does this compare with their perceptions of your competitors? How can you change perceptions and how do you measure the effectiveness of the programme?

brilliant example

Companies like IBM, Dell and Sony stand for stability, flexibility and innovation, values that give them strength in the marketplace. Positioning can sometimes be counterproductive. Apple's emphasis on cool design gave it a different positioning compared with an IBM or Microsoft which corporate buyers saw as solid and reliable.

Review capability

present your capability in a way that is relevant to your customers

Ensure that you present your capability in a way that is relevant to your customers. Assess your strengths and weaknesses to identify areas where you may need to improve your own performance. These are some of the issues you should consider:

- What strengths and benefits do you bring to your customers?
- What do they need to know to evaluate you as a supplier?
- How can you ensure that your customers always have up-to-date information on your capability?

brilliant tip

There are a number of factors that customers might use to assess your capability. Use customer requirements to identify the messages you need to include in any positioning statements:

- Commitment to your business.
- Your future direction.
- Market experience.
- Technical expertise.

- Management capability.
- Company resources.
- Financial stability.
- Policy of collaboration.

Commitment to the business

Demonstrate that you have invested in the future growth and development of your business. You have a long-term plan for the business, and there are no internal or external factors that will adversely affect your performance or commitment to that activity. You have a statement of direction which shows how you plan to develop the business over the long term and you can demonstrate that you have the resources to achieve that development. You have a record of innovation and excellence and you are highly regarded by customers and competitors. Your customer base contains a high proportion of long-term customers. You may be involved in industry associations or in collaborative projects which demonstrate that you are prepared to make a major contribution to the future of your industry.

Your future direction

What plans do you have for growth, and what shape will the business have in, say, five years' time? Information on your future product or service range will help your customers develop their own long-term plans. If, for example, you are planning to develop technological or market leadership, or if you are planning to expand your activities on an international scale, your customers will be able to take advantage of your future facilities or capabilities.

Market experience

Your track record is a key factor in positioning. You are showing that you are capable of understanding your customers' requirements and that you have already developed successful solutions in that market. You may be the market leader or you may have a growing market share. Your market knowledge may be specialised – focused on specific niche markets or sectors which are of interest to your partner.

Technical expertise

Providing examples of technical innovation or leadership is one method of demonstrating capability, but customers are also interested in your potential for future development. Your annual expenditure on research and development, your record in new product development and your technical and research resources help to substantiate your claims of technical expertise. The quality and experience of your technical staff and their ability to work closely with other technical teams will help to produce collaborative solutions for your customers.

Management capability

Your customers will want to know that you have the resources to manage your business effectively and ensure that they are provided with the highest standards of service. You have an experienced management team and you have a management training and development programme in position to ensure that your managers are continually developing their skills to meet changing business requirements. Your managers have the right level of experience in the customer's market sector and understand their requirements.

Company resources

To demonstrate that you can sustain long-term commitment to your customers, you must prove that you have the resources to provide the level of service customers need, now and in the future. What are the key facts about your company – your size, number of employees, location, turnover and profitability, national or international network and your infrastructure. This will help your customers decide whether you can handle their target level of business. For example, if your customers operate a national or international network of branches, do you have a corresponding network to meet their local needs? Do you have the production resources to handle increasing volumes of business and can you invest or automate any processes to increase your capacity? How many staff have you got, and are you using training to develop their skills?

Financial stability

Customers need to have confidence that you can continue to provide them with the same high standards of service over the long term. If there are any doubts about your financial stability, they may not wish to commit themselves to your company as a sole supplier. Make sure that your customers have a full understanding of the financial structure and performance of your company. If your company is part of a larger group, explain the financial relationship and use the strength of the group's financial resources to demonstrate your own stability. Describe any major investment programmes that you are carrying out and provide your customers with regular information on your financial performance.

Policy of collaboration

Quote other examples of collaboration that you have been involved in. Describe the key success factors and show how you have used your capabilities to ensure the success of your customers' projects. By demonstrating involvement in user groups or industry liaison committees, you can also show that you are capable of working closely with other people to achieve joint objectives.

Develop corporate branding messages

brilliant tip

Corporate branding messages give customers and prospects the confidence to buy from a company. They demonstrate that a company has the capability, resources and financial stability to operate as a viable, long-term supplier or business partner. Corporate branding is a powerful way of addressing the net impact of a company's whole activities.

Branding messages communicate the personality and promise of a company to its target market. They focus on the positive aspects of a company to build a strong corporate reputation. The key elements of corporate reputation, as we described in the previous section, are financial stability, sound management, clear vision, technical excellence, market leadership, commitment to innovation, skilled employees and excellent investment record.

> branding messages communicate the personality and promise of a company

Creating a branding roadmap

A corporate brand messaging roadmap is a useful tool for planning communications to support your positioning. The roadmap begins with an audit of your strengths and an assessment of the information needs of different members of the target audience. You can use the roadmap planning process to identify messages that differentiate you from competitors and align the messages with factors that are important to customers and other stakeholders.

Communicate the benefits of change

If your company is going through structural change, you will benefit from communicating effective corporate branding messages. Customers and other stakeholders may be uncertain about the outcome of organisational change, particularly after a merger or acquisition. Branding messages can reassure them about your future direction.

Develop a positioning strategy

Corporate branding messages can reposition a company in the marketplace by changing customer perceptions.

brilliant example

Korean electronics manufacturer Samsung moved up the value chain by changing its image from supplier of budget products under various brand names to manufacturer of innovative, high quality consumer products, grouped under a single powerful brand.

A corporate positioning strategy provides a clear advantage in the marketplace when it creates the impression that a company and its products have few credible substitutes. Positioning first gained credibility in the 1970s when Al Ries and Jack Trout wrote a series of articles on the 'positioning era' in *Advertising Age*. They summarise the technique in the phrase: 'Positioning is not what you do to a product. Positioning is what you do to the mind of the prospect.'

Gain recognition in the marketplace

Clear corporate positioning is an important determinant of market success. When you have established recognition and trust in the marketplace, you are likely to obtain more sales opportunities. You will gain the status of a pre-approved supplier in any purchasing decisions, increasing the chances of success. Clear corporate positioning helps to determine the prices you can charge and the resulting profit margins.

Customers want to buy more from a company with a good image and they will pay more for its products. A corporate positioning strategy delivers a wide range of benefits. It creates clarity and alignment within the company and differentiates a company enabling it to compete on issues other than price. It also helps the company to win business more easily and it may reduce selling costs.

> customers want to buy more from a company with a good image

Achieve clarity

Companies have to work hard to define their corporate positioning. Developing a brand positioning strategy forces a company to consider what it needs to do to be successful. The strategy should define the target market where you compete and the challenges the market faces. It should highlight the solutions you offer to those challenges and the key benefits that differentiate your company.

Align the company with the positioning

brilliant dos and donts

To use a positioning strategy effectively, you need to align your products, customer service and its people with the strategy. That is essential to proving the differentiated benefits to the customer. Simply using the positioning strategy to develop advertising slogans or corporate mission statements is not sufficient.

Work with all levels of staff to ensure they are aligned with the positioning strategy goals and understand the part they can play to achieve the position. One approach is to develop a series of key messages based on the positioning strategy and share them with all customer-facing staff. This will ensure that staff communicate consistently in every customer contact and reinforce the corporate positioning.

Develop key messages

brilliant definition

Key message

Key messages provide your company with a clear framework for communication. They set out the facts that differentiate your company from competitors and communicate benefits that are important to the target audience. Key messages are crucial to the success of marketing communications.

Research perceptions

Carry out research to assess how the target audience currently perceives your company. Identify the target perceptions that will persuade the target audience to hold a positive and favourable attitude towards your company. Audit existing communications to identify current messaging. Compare the current position with target perceptions and set objectives for developing key messages.

Position clearly

Position the company clearly in the minds of the target audience. This is also known as a positioning statement. Develop key messages that explain exactly what the company does. Set out the company's mission and core values. Describe achievements that demonstrate leadership in the market. Provide proof points for any claims.

Differentiate

Identify the factors that differentiate your company. Relate the messages to the most important issues and challenges facing the target audience. Develop key messages that align with the factors customers consider when making purchasing decisions. Use proof points to make comparisons with competitors, quoting independent authorities where possible.

Communicate value

Describe how your company's products or services benefit the target audience. This is also known as a value proposition. Translate product features into benefits for the audience. Create relevant value propositions for different members of the target audience such as business, technical or financial decision makers. Use research to align key messages with the information needs of each group.

Create a messaging framework

Publish a framework for key messages. This is the equivalent of a corporate identity manual for messages. Issue the framework to all customer-facing staff and teams from marketing agencies. Use the framework to ensure consistent use of key messages in all communications and improve the results from marketing programmes. Create message templates for standard text used in press releases, presentations and marketing publications.

Monitor communications

Set up a procedure for reviewing and approving the key message content of all communications material before publication. Carry out continuous research to measure the effectiveness of the key message programme. Compare perceptions with the baseline at the outset of the programme.

Marketing plan in brief

Current situation

- The company is perceived as a supplier of commodity products.
- Strengths of established customer relationships.
- Weaknesses of poor corporate perception.
- Threat of shrinking market share.
- Opportunity to reinvigorate the corporate image.

Market requirements

- The market is looking for innovative suppliers that can deliver quality solutions.

Objectives

- Increase sales to existing customers.
- Take the company into new market sectors.
- Open new revenue streams.
- Counter competitive activity.
- Support a long-term business development strategy.

Strategy

- Research customer perceptions of the company to establish a benchmark.
- Develop corporate branding messages.
- Build and implement a corporate positioning strategy.
- Develop key messages.

Financial requirements

- Budget to run communications programme.

Communications

- Customer communications and briefings.
- Web content.
- Thought leadership.

Metrics

- Changes in customer perception.
- Increase in market share.
- Return on marketing investment.

brilliant recap

- Assess customers' perception of the company and compare it with your target perception.

- Develop corporate branding messages that reflect your target perception.

- Build a positioning strategy to change customers' perceptions.

- Develop key messages that reinforce the target perception and include them in all communications.

CHAPTER 6

Take your business online

Conventional distribution channels of wholesalers, retailers and other intermediaries provide a sound basis for taking products to market. However, customer preference for the convenience and price benefits of purchasing online is driving business to consider new channels to market.

Online business and marketing strategy

Taking your business online can help to meet many different aspects of your marketing strategy. These are some examples:

- Improve cost and efficiency of distribution.
- Enhance customer service.
- Increase market penetration.
- Change product or market strategy.

Set distribution objectives

Improve cost and efficiency of distribution

How well does your current channel cover the market? Does it reach all potential customers? Does it deliver products and services cost effectively? Take the car market as an example.

brilliant example

The traditional way to buy a new car was to visit a dealership where sales representatives help customers choose the right model. Ford became the first car manufacturer to sell online direct to customers. The customer requests a car; it's delivered to a local dealership and driven away. That is convenient for the customer and reduces the cost of sale, but it also removes the interactive relationship between sales representative and customer.

Enhance customer service

Opening new channels can enhance customer service. Do your customers find it convenient to use existing channels? How could you change channels to offer options that meet their preferences? In the financial services sector, products are increasingly sold through major retailers and other third parties rather than traditional outlets. By 2010, 50 per cent of European mortgages were sold through indirect channels, reflecting consumer preferences for phone and internet distribution.

Increase market penetration

developing an
e-commerce strategy
can give you access to
a global marketplace

Could a new channel increase penetration of your target markets? Do new channels reduce the barriers to market entry? Are competitors using new channels to build a strong market position? Developing an e-commerce strategy, for example, can give you access to a global marketplace.

brilliant tip

By trading online, you can target new customers worldwide and grow your business on a global scale without setting up expensive overseas operations.

Change product or market strategy

A new channel could enable you to change your product strategy and open a new range of revenue opportunities. The development of electronic books (e-books), for example, and the new generation of reading devices is changing the form and potential of books and other publications. Although an e-book is a digital delivery channel for a book, it also gives publishers the opportunity to offer customers a range of other chargeable services, increasing revenue and profit potential, as well as customer loyalty. As an example, the e-book reading device could provide revenue-generating services such as:

- Multimedia content related to the book.
- Advertising and sponsorship.
- Offers from companies with products or services relevant to the book.
- Online reader reviews.
- Links to book clubs with special offers.
- Subscription services to other digital media.
- Online purchase of digital products and services.

Meet customer needs

How well do distribution channels meet customer needs? With customers showing an increasing preference for buying online, can you adapt your strategy to meet their needs? New distribution channels offer opportunities in five key areas:

- Online purchasing.
- Niche products.
- Universal access.
- Digital distribution.
- Customer support.

Implement online purchasing

What's the level of online purchasing in your market sector? More than 875 million consumers worldwide shopped online in

more than 875 million consumers worldwide shopped online in 2010

2010 – that's an increase of 40 per cent in just two years. In the United States alone, e-commerce sales for 2010 were estimated at $165.4 billion, an increase of 14.8 per cent from 2009, while total retail sales in 2010 increased just 7 per cent for the same period. The most popular online purchases are high volume products – books, clothing, accessories and shoes, and videos, DVDs and games.

brilliant definition

e-commerce

This is how the e-commerce process works:

- Customers visit your website anytime, during or outside normal business hours.
- They view products and brief descriptions.
- They select products and put them into an electronic shopping basket.
- Customers are offered payment options, ideally in their own currency.

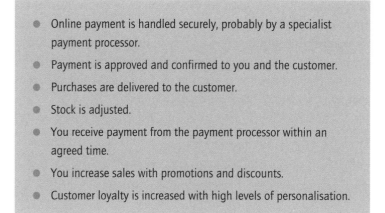

- Online payment is handled securely, probably by a specialist payment processor.
- Payment is approved and confirmed to you and the customer.
- Purchases are delivered to the customer.
- Stock is adjusted.
- You receive payment from the payment processor within an agreed time.
- You increase sales with promotions and discounts.
- Customer loyalty is increased with high levels of personalisation.

Software to run an e-commerce site is available off the shelf. This may be suitable if you are just starting e-commerce operations or if your volumes are expected to be low. However, for more complex sites, a purpose-built solution may be more appropriate. You also have to decide whether to operate the site yourself or use a specialist company to host the site for you.

Market niche products

Do you have products that sell in small volume? Using the internet as a channel opens new revenue and profit opportunities by offering consumers a wider choice of niche products. When customers recognise that they can find the products they want online, market advantage will switch from companies with bestsellers to those offering a wider product choice. In the book market, for example, customers are frequently looking for titles that are out of print.

Low inventory costs combined with cumulative sales across a range of niche products make this an attractive opportunity. Small businesses thrive in the long tail because they need only a relatively small number of people to be interested in what they offer compared with mass-market companies which need audiences of millions to be profitable. The key is to make the entire range available and help customers find what they want. That means understanding how people buy, recognising what they're looking for and making it clear in all your marketing materials that you can make it easy for them to find it.

Provide access anytime, anywhere

Consumers in the internet generation expect the convenience of shopping whenever and wherever they want it.

- They expect round-the-clock availability.
- They want easily accessible information.
- They favour high levels of self-service.
- They need simple secure payment facilities.

Creating a website with online purchasing facilities is an essential starting point, but you also need to develop plans for delivering information, services and products over other increasingly popular channels such as mobile phones. The latest smartphones offer powerful computing and web browsing facilities, creating a new, potentially large distribution channel. Take advantage of the contactless payment facilities that are available on smartphones. Contactless payment, in which a consumer swipes a payment unit with their mobile phone, provides a fast, convenient method of paying for small purchases. According to a study by market research company IMS Research, the number of locations that accept contactless payments is set to increase by over 12.5 million by the end of 2013.

Offer digital distribution

Digital distribution offers an opportunity to speed delivery, reduce logistics and stockholding costs and improve customer convenience.

E-ticketing is an example of a new channel strategy that benefits both customers and suppliers. E-ticketing is rapidly replacing traditional paper tickets. It is particularly important for the entertainment business and the travel industry where an e-ticket is used to represent the purchase of a seat, usually through a website or by telephone. Once a reservation is made, an e-ticket exists only as a digital record in the issuer's computers. Customers usually print out a copy of their receipt which contains the reservation number and the e-ticket number.

To check in with an e-ticket, the customer usually comes to the check-in counter and presents the confirmation or reservation code. For customers this means stress-free ticketing, no tickets to lose and no last minute queues for tickets. For suppliers, electronic ticketing will allow them greater opportunities to manage the corporate travel experience by being able to make changes to the actual ticket while the customer is on the telephone. For airlines, it is estimated that approximately US$9 in savings could be made when an electronic ticket is issued instead of a paper ticket.

Deliver customer support

Do you provide customer support via a helpdesk or field support team? The internet provides an opportunity to reduce the cost of delivering customer support by providing online self-service facilities for simpler support issues.

Online video, for example, creates a powerful sales and customer support tool. By demonstrating the product in action, you can help visitors get a better understanding of the potential benefits of the product and remove some of the risk from their purchase decision. A video demonstration is particularly useful for communicating features and benefits that would be difficult to explain or understand with words and pictures. Online video can also help to improve customer service and reduce your support costs. By providing online video clips showing how to use products or how to resolve faults, you can allow customers to help themselves.

---

brilliant timesaver

Companies that set up internet forums frequently find that customers are helping each other. Customers post technical questions or service queries on the forum and receive answers, either from company support staff or from other customers who have experienced the same problems. This not only reduces the burden on the helpdesk, it also helps to build community and strengthen customer loyalty.

Operate a multi-channel strategy

By opening new distribution channels and operating a multi-channel strategy you can offer customers greater choice as well as increase your own marketing flexibility. New channels offer significant benefits, but they may not be appropriate for your business. You are moving into an entirely new business and you must be certain that there are real benefits. Most important, you must take a realistic view of the opportunities and threats. You may need to recruit people with the skills to manage an e-business. Traditional management skills may not be appropriate to a 24-hour business with new customer expectations and new forms of competition. Managing a strategy like this requires a new approach to channel management. There are a number of important requirements:

- Drive business to the new channels.
- Maintain consistent standards of quality and performance across all channels.

- Brand different channels consistently.
- Provide a 360 degree view of all channel transactions for your sales and customer service teams.
- Consider a differential pricing strategy for different channels.
- Set up payment mechanisms.

Drive business to the new channels

If your new channel strategy is to succeed, you need to make customers aware of the existence and benefits of the channels. There are a number of important tasks:

- Send emails to existing customers to alert them to the new channel. Make an introductory offer for initial purchases.
- Announce the new channels with press releases to relevant consumer or trade publications.
- Promote the new channels on your website.
- Integrate messages about the new channel into your other marketing campaigns to raise awareness.

Maintain consistent standards of quality and performance across all channels

Delivering quality of service is vital. Customers will expect a prompt response from all your channels and that means reliable operation, available 24 hours a day, 7 days a week. Once customers are on your website, you must provide a quality internet shopping experience. Simple navigation, clear product information, extensive self-service facilities and easy ordering and payment are essential. If customers need help, support should be available, online or via the telephone.

Mobile commerce services present additional challenges. Customers who want to shop online using their smartphones will be looking at product information and placing orders via a small screen and cramped keyboard. Make sure that content is redesigned for mobile screens and create simple ordering procedures that require a minimum number of keystrokes.

brilliant dos and don'ts

Brand channels consistently

Opening new distribution channels offers you greater marketing flexibility. However, it can also fragment your brand identity. Ensure that all channels reflect the same identity in their use of logos, typefaces, visual images and marketing messages. Customers may become confused if they receive conflicting identities and messages.

Provide a 360 degree view of all channel transactions for your sales and customer service teams

Most companies have detailed customer records, but how many are aware of all the customer interactions that take place? Very few have a 360 degree view of the customer, that is, a single view of all customer interactions. The 360 degree view tells you how your customers are contacting you, browsing your website, acquiring information, ordering products, placing service enquiries or making complaints. It brings together all this information to build a detailed profile and it shows how well your channels match your customers' activities.

Getting a 360 degree view is essential if you want to optimise marketing, communications, customer service and product development. Used effectively, the 360 degree view strengthens customer retention and can increase customers' lifetime value and profitability. Looking ahead, once you have built a 360 degree view, you can tailor products and services to

> used effectively, the 360 degree view strengthens customer retention

meet customers' long-term needs, confident that you have a complete picture.

The 360 degree approach underpins a number of important customer service initiatives:

- It supports the development of measurable goals, objectives and tactics for every point of interaction customers have with your company.
- It establishes company-wide business metrics, customer measurement, tracking and reporting processes for all sectors, product lines and points of contact.
- It helps to create customer interaction guidelines that span every part of your company that has customer contact.

The 360 degree approach is based on networking technologies that integrate information from separate departments and IT systems. However, it is the people who interact with customers who deliver the real benefits. They must be committed to the single point of contact approach and they must be able to use the full facilities of the system so that they are able to deliver prompt, quality service and recognise opportunities to win new business.

Consider a differential pricing strategy for different channels

The internet has made pricing strategy a more critical element in the marketing mix. Price transparency means that customers can easily find out what it will cost to buy the same product or service at a range of different outlets. Although customers have accepted in the past that prices vary by region and location, they are now able to overcome the barriers of distance and find the lowest price. That means static pricing models are no longer appropriate. Where price is one of the main considerations in a pricing decision, your online pricing must respond to competitive pricing levels.

> static pricing models are no longer appropriate

Set up payment mechanisms

An effective payment system allows your customers to buy through your online channels and allows you to manage the process efficiently. A complete payment system includes all the facilities to display products, accept payments and manage your business.

- Display products that customers can buy from the channel.
- Display and change prices, discounts and special offers in multiple currencies.
- Calculate any taxes due.
- Calculate shipping or delivery charges.
- Provide a quick, simple ordering mechanism.
- Provide a secure customer payment mechanism for multiple currencies.
- Accept payment by credit card, debit card and cheque.
- Handle transactions from customers with approved accounts.
- Handle customer refunds.
- Automate stock control.
- Simplify administration and accounting.

You can set up your own payment processing facilities. However, if you handle only a small number of transactions, or if your transaction requirements are complex, this may not be a practical proposition. Payment processors can provide you with an established proven system that can grow in line with your business. Payment processing services are available from banks or independent specialists.

Marketing plan in brief

Current situation

- Current distribution through bricks-and-mortar retailers.
- Strength of face-to-face customer relationships.
- Weakness of changing market requirements.
- Threat of price competition from online retailers.
- Opportunity to extend market coverage.

Market requirements

- Consumer preference for convenience of online purchasing.
- Demand for lower online prices.

Objectives

- Improve cost and efficiency of distribution.
- Enhance customer service.
- Increase market penetration.
- Change product or market strategy.

Strategy

- Implement online purchasing.
- Offer digital distribution.
- Operate multi-channel strategy.

Financial requirements

- Develop online pricing plan.

▶

Communications

● Raise customer awareness.

● Drive business to online channels.

Metrics

● Increase in overall sales, revenue or profit generated by the new channel.

● Proportion of sales to existing customers moving to the new channel.

● Sales to new customers via the new channel.

● Gains from competitive accounts via the new channel.

● Market penetration enabled by the new channel.

● Changes in customer satisfaction levels.

● Customer channel preferences.

brilliant recap

● Set cost, service and marketing objectives for your new channel.

● Make sure the new channel meets your customers' needs for convenience and service.

● Operate a multi-channel strategy to offer your customers greater choice.

● Set up a differential pricing strategy to match conditions in each channel.

CHAPTER 7

Make the most of social media

Social networking in business is not a new phenomenon, however the rapid growth of tools such as Twitter, Facebook and LinkedIn has changed the way social networking is used. Instead of being used just for internal communication, social networking tools are now being used as a way of engaging directly with customers – releasing news, marketing products or raising the company profile. Ignoring Twitter and other social media overlooks an important channel of communication.

Social media and marketing strategy

Social media can help to meet many different aspects of your marketing strategy. These are some examples:

- Improve communication with customers and prospects.
- Strengthen relationships with customers.
- Position the company in different ways.

Use a mainstream medium

Although Twitter was only launched in 2006, it now has millions of users and is regarded as a vital medium of communication throughout

Twitter is a vital medium of communication throughout the world the world. The power of the medium to deliver information quickly was reinforced in 2009 when a New York resident used Twitter to break the news about the Hudson River plane crash 15 minutes before any traditional news medium was aware of the event. Events like that have made Twitter as widely used as email, mobile phones and other social networks.

Develop a business tool

brilliant definition

Twitter

Twitter is now regarded as a mainstream business tool. Although the format is limited, the 140-character 'tweets' can be used for many forms of marketing activity, including raising awareness, improving customer relationships, promoting events, encouraging feedback and tracking customer/competitor activities. It provides a short, immediate form of communication that can be used for delivering time-critical messages quickly or for directing people to more detailed information on a website or other medium.

Commentators have highlighted the fact that business users are also consumers and expect to use applications like Twitter at work just as they would at home. The expectations of business users have changed dramatically, and these users are becoming more demanding about the look, feel and speed of communications.

Speak to customers directly

Twitter allows your business to speak to a wide range of people for free and to place a link in the text so that users can look for further information. Although this might be difficult if you operate in a high volume market, using Twitter allows you to speak directly to each customer or prospect. By using the search facility it is possible to see who is talking about your products and your market. That can also help you to identify prospects.

Direct traffic to your website

The links that you can embed in tweets can be used to drive traffic to your website. This can be useful if you are launching a new product, announcing important changes or making a special offer and want to provide detailed information quickly.

brilliant example

Communications networking company Cisco Systems uses Twitter to alert customers to the availability of new presentations or white papers on their website. This improves the distribution and take-up of thought leadership material and increases frequency of customer contact.

Monitor market activity

Twitter users often link to useful websites or articles that can provide a source of valuable information about activities in your marketplace. You can also subscribe to Twitter feeds for specific websites or conferences, allowing you to receive and view content quickly.

Notify customers quickly

You can set up a Twitter feed to notify customers of important developments such as new products, service information, management changes, product recalls or special customer offers. Customers can subscribe to the alerts via a mobile phone messaging service or an RSS facility in their email programme for instant notification. Twitter can also be used to provide personalised updates for individual customers.

brilliant tip

Update visitors during an event

If you are organising an event such as a seminar or exhibition, you can use Twitter to inform participants of any important changes, results or findings. For example, you might want to let delegates know that an important presentation is about to start or that there will be a special offer during the event.

Create and measure new revenue streams

Some companies have found that Twitter can become an important additional revenue stream through its ability to constantly update followers with the latest product news. As an example, when a local outlet wants to make a special offer because it has excess stock, placing an advert in a newspaper that appears days later may be expensive and not quick enough. Twitter announcements happen immediately and go direct to the customers and prospects who are interested. By tracking the revenue that results from Twitter postings or Twitter-generated visits to a main website, you can calculate the contribution that Twitter makes.

Find more prospects

Twitter can be used to identify potential customers. By searching for keywords related to your product on Twitter Search, you can identify and follow users with similar product interests. You can then tweet about topics related to your own product and follow up with direct messages or other forms of communication.

Provide new forms of customer support

An increasing number of companies are using Twitter to help customers with support issues. Support specialists monitor online conversations on their website about ongoing product or service problems, then post messages to direct the users to the appropriate support resources.

brilliant example

Train operating company London Midland provides passengers with regular updates on how trains are running, travel advice, and information on current and future promotions. The company also uses Twitter to alert passengers to service disruption while they are travelling.

Encourage customer comment

Twitter can be used as a social networking platform for interacting with customers, colleagues and business partners as an integral element of a customer and partner relationship management programme: that gives it an important role in company strategy. One company reported a 30 per cent decline in negative comments after recognising that it was able to solve more customer issues through social media such as Twitter.

Involve customers in product development

Progressive companies are taking customer interaction a stage further and encouraging customers and other people to submit brief product or business ideas via Twitter, with a facility for other users to give their views on the ideas. Customers know what they want from a new product and companies can use social media like Twitter to listen to those views and to act upon them. This can reduce costs associated with product development as well as create a focus group that can provide feedback on new developments. A degree of involvement like this may also create a higher level of expectation, demand and acceptance when a new product is launched.

Provide information for the media

Journalists, industry analysts and other researchers use Twitter to gather information for projects or stories they are writing. By providing useful information in your tweets, you can build an informed group of followers and improve the coverage given to your company.

Manage the use of Twitter

Twitter can act as a powerful tool that can help you manage the environment where your product or brand is discussed. However, you need to make users aware of your brand, and the key is to attract users from the Twitter site to your own website and focus on getting a measurable return from the medium. It's also important to set guidelines to cover interaction with customers. If you put a message on Twitter, you have to make sure it is clear that the information is from your company. There are strong rules of etiquette on Twitter and breaking them can create an adverse reaction.

As more companies recognise the importance of Twitter for interacting with customers, customer relationship management (CRM) system vendors are launching new products to help companies manage their Twitter activities. Software is commercially available that enables companies to monitor Twitter conversations online and engage with users by responding to relevant messages.

Deliver measurable results

As with any other medium, you should set objectives for Twitter and, where possible, make these measurable. Experience so far indicates that it is possible to measure actual revenue resulting from Twitter posts.

brilliant example

Dell uses Twitter to alert customers to sales and other special offers. In 2009, the company reported that Twitter posts directing customers to offers on its website had generated over $1 million of additional revenue in the previous 18 months.

Introduce video marketing

Video marketing enables you to add an increasingly popular medium to your online marketing programme. You can use video to demonstrate products, provide instructions for use, share endorsements or communicate through webcasts.

brilliant dos and don'ts

Although you can create online video for relatively low production and distribution costs, you should not sacrifice quality. Like any other marketing tool, online video must build a quality brand image.

Take advantage of a highly effective communication medium. A website page with video is 50 times more likely than a text-only page to feature on the first page of search engine rankings. Video is also growing in popularity as an online medium, with video now the highest proportion of broadband traffic.

a website page with video is 50 times more likely than a text-only page to feature on the first page of search engine rankings

Demonstrate products

Use online video to demonstrate your products. Show the product in action and encourage website visitors to leave feedback. Online video is ideal for products that require demonstration to highlight benefits, or products where simplicity of use is an important selling point. Encourage satisfied customers to provide endorsements or reviews on video. Post them on the product pages and provide facilities for visitors to upload their own video feedback or leave other forms of feedback. Use video to encourage visitors to take action by visiting detailed product pages, looking for more information or ordering online.

Provide video support

Create instructional videos to show customers how to use a product. This can build customer satisfaction by ensuring that customers make effective use of their purchase. It also helps to reduce support costs by providing a cost-effective alternative to a helpdesk.

Encourage interaction

Put thought leadership online. Publish videos of round table discussions on issues relevant to customers. Create video interviews with industry experts talking about future trends or other key topics. Encourage interaction by inviting visitors to post questions or leave feedback.

Manage the programme

Make your videos easy to find. Put keywords in the title so that search engines can locate and rank the content. Embed the videos on product pages on your own website or upload them on sites such as YouTube.

Measure the effectiveness of your video campaign. Track the number of visitors and length of time visitors spend on a site. Identify any online sales that result from a visitor viewing a video. Compare the number of support calls to a helpdesk before and after the launch of an instructional video.

Manage your online reputation

Businesses find it harder than ever to control their reputation online. Blogs, product review sites and social networking tools give anyone with internet access a platform for voicing their opinion on your products or your business. The increasing number of online channels makes it difficult to monitor what people are saying. If people are making negative comments this can damage your reputation, so it is essential to track comments, respond positively and take any necessary remedial action. If the scale of the task becomes difficult, consider hiring a firm specialising in online reputation management.

Monitor channels

Identify the channels where people are talking about your business. Monitor search engines to find references to your company, product or brand names. The references could be in press, radio or television items, blogs, social media sites, forum posts and websites of other companies.

brilliant tip

Check the search engine rankings to see how high any negative references appear.

Respond

Respond to any criticisms or suggestions. Acknowledge the author of the comments and thank them for highlighting any issues. Respect any valid criticism and promise to deal with the issue. Describe any remedial action you plan to take with a timescale for improvement. Identify any individuals that you feel warrant a personal response. This can help to create good-will and that may result in positive feedback and comments in the future.

Take any necessary remedial action. If critics highlight product issues, identify product development tasks to improve performance or usability. If service issues are the problem, review your customer service operations and identify opportunities for improvement. Prioritise any problems that are generating high levels of comment.

Build dialogue

Build dialogue on the relevant channels. Post your own comments on blogs and forums to communicate your opinions on hot topics and demonstrate your willingness to engage. Set up forums, communities or review facilities on your own website to encourage further dialogue.

Counter

Counter unfair or damaging online references content by publishing positive content. A high proportion of people will click on a negative result if it appears just below a company website in search engine rankings. Publishing your own positive content will help push the negative material further down the rankings and reduce its search engine visibility and impact.

Marketing plan in brief

Current situation

- Customer communications through traditional channels.
- Strengths of regular customer contact.
- Weakness of no communications through emerging social media channels.
- Threats of lack of control over customer communication channels.
- Opportunity to build dialogue and improve customer relationships.

Market requirements

- Communication through preferred social media channels.

Objectives

- Improve communication with customers and prospects.
- Strengthen relationships with customers.
- Position the company in different ways.

Strategy

- Use mainstream business social media.
- Monitor online communications.
- Provide new forms of online customer support.
- Introduce video marketing tools.
- Manage your online reputation.

Financial requirements

- Investment in customer support facilities.

▶

Communications

- Adapt existing communications to social media.

Metrics

- Customer satisfaction levels.
- Changes in customer support costs.
- Changes in level of complaints.

brilliant recap

- Adopt social media like Twitter which are now mainstream business media.

- Identify ways to use social media to improve communications with customers.

- Provide new forms of customer support using social media and online resources.

- Introduce video marketing to improve campaign impact.

- Manage your reputation online and build dialogue with customers and critics.

PART 3

Sales channels

CHAPTER 8

Improve
sales force
performance

The performance of the sales force plays an important role in determining the success of your marketing strategy. Historically, the sales force has been used tactically to maximise sales potential and to deal almost exclusively with the purchasing department. However, changing purchasing patterns and a focus on customer relationships are changing that traditional role from sales representative to account manager. The change in the sales force has been described as 'from hunter to farmer', and it may take more than simple training to achieve this. Sales automation is providing a further boost to sales force productivity and performance.

Sales force performance and marketing strategy

Improving sales force performance contributes to the achievement of many marketing objectives, including:

- Increase sales to existing customers.
- Develop sales to new customers.
- Increase account control.
- Strengthen long-term customer relationships.
- Improve customer focus.
- Influence purchasing patterns.
- Control sales costs.
- Counter competitive activity.

Change the role of the sales force

There are a number of important elements bringing about a change in the role from sales representative to account manager:

- Shift from short-term sales to managing customer relations.
- Need to understand the customer's whole business.
- Need to develop a long-term focus.
- Move from individual account responsibility to team working.
- Need to work at different levels in the customer organisation.
- Need to understand and influence the complete decision-making structure.
- Recognition of the importance of customer care and customer satisfaction.
- Growing understanding of the need for complete business solutions.

Manage customer relationships

brilliant definition

Account management

The traditional sales team focus is on sales, with recognition of the importance of profit. However, in account management the responsibility should be much wider, with the emphasis on managing relationships. Sales representatives should be asking:

- Are we dealing with all the key decision makers and influencers?
- What can we do to build stronger relationships with our customers?
- How can we improve delivery or product quality in line with the needs of our customers?
- Is the company delivering the highest standards of satisfaction?

Building customer relationships is a time-consuming process and that can pose problems for sales people who are used to improving sales productivity – achieving the highest levels of turnover for the minimum investment of time. Meeting other decision makers, reviewing progress on technical projects, making proactive customer care visits, arranging meetings between different members of the account team and briefing other specialists within the company are tasks that a traditional sales person would regard as distractions from the main task of selling. For years, the pressure has been on to minimise the time spent on travelling or administration in order to increase sales productivity, and suddenly the sales force is asked to handle a whole range of other assignments. It is vital that the sales people understand the importance of these activities and do not regard them as a waste of time.

> building customer relationships can pose problems for sales people who are used to improving sales productivity

Understand the customer's whole business

The sales people must widen their understanding of the customer's business. In a traditional sales environment, their focus would be on the purchasing department and on the immediate requirement for their products. Account management requires a much broader understanding:

- What is the customer's business?
- What are its requirements?
- How is the company doing?
- What are the company's success factors?
- How can we help customers to improve their business?
- What other business opportunities are there apart from current product sales?
- Who needs to be influenced to realise these business opportunities?

This level of business understanding requires a much greater appreciation of business than the basic sales techniques, and again the sales people should not feel they are wasting their time in acquiring this knowledge.

Transform a sales force into an account team

To make the transition to the account team, the sales people have to acquire a broad range of new skills, including project management, communications skills, customer care, presentation skills and team management. The account team should be a major contributor to new business development and the achievement of the highest levels of customer satisfaction. It can also represent a considerable cost factor which requires constant review and enhanced strategies to ensure it adds value to the customer relationship.

There are two main roles within an account team:

● Account support, which should be focused on the complete service delivered to the customer and maximising customer satisfaction levels.

● Account development, which should be focused on pre-sales support and the development of the business.

sales managers should operate a skills development programme

By developing the right level of skills to support each role, sales managers can maintain the highest levels of account team productivity and ensure that customers receive a consistently high standard of service. Sales managers should operate a skills development programme to enable:

● Penetration and development of targeted accounts, utilising business and industry skills.

- Achievement of account revenue growth and market leadership.
- An increase in account team productivity.
- Greater improvements in individual performance.

Identify success factors in account management

The successful development of the account management role depends on a number of factors:

- Effective working relationships between different members of the team.
- The development of the right skill base to meet the job requirements.
- A continuing drive to improve account team productivity.
- Management commitment to the account team's role, with opportunities for career progression.
- Reinforcement of the role through authorised career structures, job descriptions and core training programmes.

The account manager needs to:

- Understand the customer's needs.
- Translate them into product and service requirements.
- Ensure the rest of the company understands those requirements.
- Deliver a solution that meets those requirements.
- Identify and meet future requirements.

Develop account management skills

If we look at the areas that need to be addressed in a major account, it becomes clear that an account manager needs a wide range of skills, including:

- Understanding the financial and legal requirements of the account.
- Understanding the company's business objectives.
- Understanding the company's commercial policies.
- Building high levels of product awareness.
- Understanding the customer's business objectives.
- Identifying key decision makers.
- Understanding the customer's purchasing strategy.
- Assessing competitive activities.
- Putting together an account development plan.
- Ensuring effective sales order processing.
- Building the right levels of revenue and profitability.

The account manager does not need to have an expert knowledge of all those areas; their role is to understand the implications and appoint appropriate specialists to provide the right balance of account skills. The account manager therefore needs a balance of personal and business skills:

- Core personal skills to meet job standards, including:
  - Delegation
  - Interpersonal skills
  - Consultancy
  - Financial control and analysis
  - Project management
  - Man management
  - Initiative and creativity.
- Secondary skills to meet business and customer requirements, such as industry, competitive and product knowledge.

Set challenging objectives for the account team

The objective of account development is to achieve continued growth from targeted accounts, avoiding the stop/start process of tactical selling. This is a long-term process that requires continued effort at a number of different stages:

> account development is a long-term process that requires continued effort

- Pre-sales.
- Contract negotiation.
- Implementation/delivery.
- Review.

This provides a number of different objectives for the account team:

- Ensure that the customer is presented with a coherent and professional image of your company as a business partner.
- Secure a long-term business relationship with the customer as the basis for growing business.
- Penetrate the customer's organisation and decision-making processes, creating new opportunities that can be exploited to accelerate account growth.
- Understand and document, on an ongoing basis, the customer organisation's strategic business direction and organisation.
- Provide the company's senior management team with feedback on the long-term growth potential in the customer's market sector and on the critical success factors for exploiting it.
- Ensure that the company's solutions are technically sound and based on a proper understanding of the customer's requirements.
- Ensure that the company's total resource is delivered in a way that satisfies customer requirements and supports the objectives of the account plan.

Establish duties and responsibilities

A key account manager should be responsible for the following activities within the context of the account plan and as a member of the account team.

Account development

- Understand the customer's business objectives and promote awareness within the account team.
- Promote the company's product and industry strategies within the customer's organisation.
- Help the account manager in the development, production and maintenance of the account plan.
- Influence the customer's strategy in line with the account plan.
- Develop relationships with the customer to identify new business opportunities and penetrate new departments to create new development opportunities for the company.

Sales support

- Ensure adequate resource is forecast and available to support the sales campaign. This may include technical staff, business skills or demonstration facilities.
- Inform all resource providers of the projected requirements.
- Monitor the application of resources to achieve the objectives.
- Provide a feedback to resource management on the quality of the resource provided.

Promotion and management of product sales

- Identify opportunities to maximise product revenues.
- Promote and exploit the company's products.
- Produce and maintain an up-to-date services revenue forecast and manage performance against target.

Customer satisfaction

- Ensure that customer requirements are fully understood and can be met.

- Ensure that adequate plans exist within the company to meet customer requirements.

- Ensure adequate resource is allocated to achieve the plans.

- Monitor the progress of implementation against plans.

- Portray a positive image of the company, its products and services in all dealings with the customer.

- Ensure the customer is aware that their requirements are being met.

Introduce sales automation

brilliant **timesaver**

The development of account management skills helps the sales force to make the critical change in roles. However, industry experience indicates that sales representatives spend a significant proportion of their time on non-sales activities. By automating routine administrative tasks and putting relevant information on the desktop, you can free your account team to spend more time on productive work.

Improve call productivity

Sales automation tools allow your sales representatives to identify promising leads quickly and then coordinate the account team efforts to close the deal. They help you lower your costs of sales, respond faster to customer enquiries and share information across your entire company.

example

Sales teams can use automation tools to gather up-to-the-minute customer information over the internet before calling on potential customers. They can then use this data to customise product offers or provide quotes in real time during the sales calls. They can instantly forward orders over the internet to head office. This speeds delivery and accounting processes, and increases sales teams' ability to respond to customer needs.

Enhance the whole selling process

Sales automation tools support key aspects of the selling process, including marketing, contact management, account management, prospecting, order fulfilment and customer service. By implementing internet-based sales automation tools you can:

● Streamline sales processes.

● Boost sales force knowledge.

● Enhance collaborative selling.

● Improve customer relationships.

● Reduce quote times.

● Increase sales force morale.

● Improve response to enquiries.

Streamline sales processes

Sales automation tools handle repetitive and time-consuming activities such as capturing website leads, qualifying buyers and triggering follow-up. They also make data rekeying unnecessary by automatically disseminating information to appropriate departments, which reduces errors and saves time.

Boost sales force knowledge

Online product catalogues can be updated the moment a new product or service is available. Sales representatives can access product specifications information at their fingertips. These electronic catalogues can also be set up to alert sales representatives to complementary products and promotions, immediately creating other selling opportunities. An online sales library can provide staff access to updated price lists, presentations and brochures created by your marketing department. This information can also be emailed to customers and prospects. The system can also incorporate a knowledge base which has information about product issues and modifications.

Improve focus

The system can help to improve sales force performance through the provision of comprehensive sales support information. It can provide the sales force with a wide range of information that builds a complete picture of customers and the way they respond to sales and marketing initiatives. The system can be used to provide the following information:

● Customer profile and contact information.

● Customer purchasing history.

● Any known problems.

● Individual sales or direct marketing initiatives and the response.

● Wider communications programmes or promotional activity within the customer's sector.

● Competitive activity on the account.

● Profitability of the account.

This kind of information improves productivity by focusing the sales force on the most important customers and prospects.

Enhance teamwork

All users of your sales automation system share access to a single data source, which supports better teamwork between sales, marketing and customer support. The system capabilities can be extended to include sales teams from your distribution partners.

Improve customer relationships

Sales automation systems can be configured to communicate information to your customers based on their specific needs and keep existing customers abreast of product updates. They also support online customer service, including automated help and access to information 24 hours a day, 7 days a week.

🕐 brilliant   timesaver

Reduce estimating and order processing times

Your sales representatives can use automation tools to determine customer requirements and immediately provide a complete proposal after a single meeting, cutting days or even weeks from the selling cycle. Some systems incorporate accounting links that enable the sales team to service customers faster by providing access to up-to-date information on customers' credit limits and balances, recent quotations and invoices. The system can also create estimates, orders and up-to-date price lists automatically.

Increase sales force morale

Sales automation applications reduce the time your staff spends on low-level business functions. They create a more flexible work environment by allowing employees to use the internet to access information when and where they need it, whether working from home, on the road, or in your office.

Improve response to enquiries

The system can manage incoming email enquiries using rules to scan messages for keywords and route the emails to the appropriate person. This ensures that no enquiry goes unanswered. The system can also monitor incoming email messages, identify the customer's record and attach the email to the customer record. The system can send an automatic response to the sender based on the message content so they know that you're actively investigating their enquiry.

Manage sales opportunities

Automation systems incorporate a powerful opportunity management system, so that sales managers can easily track performance and accurately forecast sales. They provide your sales managers with a range of important benefits:

- Offers real visibility into sales performance as a basis for managing and training a sales team.
- Incorporates step-by-step, repeatable sales processes that are proven to succeed.
- Provides tools the sales force needs to succeed.
- Creates collaborative sales processes that harness sales, service and partner resources to win deals.

The automated tools allow managers to apply best practice processes to increase the win ratio. Some systems include tools to evaluate success factors for an accurate probability of closing. They also create action plans that can increase the opportunity to win more deals.

> automated tools allow managers to apply best practice processes to increase the win ratio

Manage contacts effectively

The tools incorporate features that enable your sales force to manage their contact programme effectively. They provide full information on deals in progress, marketing campaigns, and open cases in one central location. Sales representatives and managers can access up-to-the-minute information from anywhere – on the desktop in the office or remotely on a laptop or other mobile device. The systems can also integrate with software such as Microsoft Outlook® or Microsoft Exchange®, allowing the sales team to synchronise contacts and calendars and to book meetings quickly and easily.

Monitor sales force productivity

Sales automation systems incorporate extensive reporting tools that enable sales managers to monitor performance and create accurate forecasts. The manager can review sales proposals in progress, wins, and lost deals. The systems provide a wide range of standard reports, including analysis of the sales pipeline, summary of leads, and performance by individual representative.

Most systems allow the sales manager to customise reports to meet their own requirements. The system can schedule reports so that sales managers automatically receive the reports they need to see based on a weekly or monthly schedule. It can also be set to trigger and distribute reports when a certain action occurs. For example, if a sales representative abandons or loses more than five opportunities in one week, the system would send a revised forecast and activity report to the sales manager for follow-up.

The reports can be used to improve sales force control by providing information on team and individual performance, sales costs and the effectiveness of sales support programmes. This information can be used as a basis for allocating sales resources, training, territory planning and developing other forms of support such as telesales.

brilliant example

The reports could be formatted to provide the following management information:

- The performance of different sales representatives.

- The overall performance of the sales team.

- The comparative performance of different sales channels such as field sales, telesales, distributors or agents.

- The impact of marketing campaigns on sales performance.

- Cost of sales.

- The effectiveness of different call patterns.

Manage sales leads

Automated processes can be used to import and manage leads from the internet. The sales manager can quickly assign leads to the appropriate sales representative and monitor follow-up. Automated alerts enable your sales manager to monitor sales progress and act quickly if there is a problem. For example, the system can automatically identify leads that have not been followed up within an agreed timescale and notify the manager by email. It also reminds the manager to schedule a follow-up call with the appropriate sales representative. This ensures that all leads are followed up in a timely way. The system can also notify the sales manager when a sales representative loses more than a specific number of deals in a given time frame, or has deals that are more than two weeks overdue for closing.

Marketing plan in brief

Current situation

- Sales force is structured to deal with customers' purchasing departments.
- Strengths of established customer relationships.
- Weakness of low levels of sales force productivity.
- Threat of competitive activity at major accounts.
- Opportunity to improve sales win ratios and sales force productivity.

Market requirements

- Need to improve sales force performance to meet changing market conditions.

Objectives

- Increase sales to existing customers.
- Develop sales to new customers.
- Increase account control.
- Strengthen long-term customer relationships.
- Improve customer focus.
- Influencing purchasing patterns.
- Control sales costs.
- Counter competitive activity.

Strategy

- Change the role of the sales force to account management.
- Manage customer relationships more effectively.
- Introduce sales automation tools.
- Manage sales opportunities more effectively.

Financial requirements

- Invest in sales automation tools.
- Budget for sales force training.

Communications

- Sales force communications to raise awareness of customer service and account management.

Metrics

- Increase in sales, revenue or profit by individual sales representative.
- Increase in sales, revenue or profit by sales force.
- Reduction in customer churn.
- Gains from competitive accounts.
- Improvement in sales force productivity.
- Increase in customer satisfaction levels.

brilliant recap

- Change the role of the sales force to account management to increase account penetration.
- Manage customer relationships more effectively.
- Introduce sales automation tools to improve sales force productivity and efficiency.
- Manage sales opportunities more effectively to close the gap between lead generation and account win.

CHAPTER 9

Reduce the sales cycle

How long does it take to go from first sales contact to purchase? What are the main customer and internal barriers to a sale? How do you close the gap between marketing and sales, and improve collaboration? How can you accelerate the sales cycle? These are challenges that sales directors face on a day-to-day basis, but they are not issues that are exclusive to sales. Marketing plays an important role in reducing the sales cycle.

Sales cycle reduction and marketing strategy

Reducing the sales cycle can help to meet many different aspects of your marketing strategy. These are some examples:

- Improve time to revenue.
- Improve return on marketing investment.
- Reduce competitive threats.
- Increase customer retention.

Analyse the buying process

Companies rarely buy products or services on impulse. The decision to buy is the result of a long process of investigation, consideration and review. Different people will evaluate prod-

most companies share a
common buying cycle

ucts and companies. To be able
to market and sell effectively and
to make the best use of your marketing resources, it's important to
understand how your customers and
prospects buy, and to recognise which stage of the cycle they
are currently in. Although your customers and prospects may
vary in size, most companies share a common buying cycle.
Those common factors can help you to determine the nature of
your sales and marketing campaign.

brilliant definition

The buying cycle

The buying cycle typically moves through four key stages:
1   Identify a business need.
2   Research a solution.
3   Design and evaluate different solutions.
4   Purchase.

Change marketing focus

The complexity of the buying process places a fundamentally
different emphasis on the role of sales and marketing teams. It's
no longer enough to base the success of a marketing campaign
on the volume of leads. The real
measure is the conversion ratio and
quality of business wins. Marketing
activity needs to go beyond stimulating interest – it has to play a crucial
part in all stages of the process until
closure. This is a process called
joined-up marketing. Joined-up marketing places a far greater
emphasis on the whole sales process, ensuring that all parties

it's no longer enough
to base the success of a
marketing campaign on
the volume of leads

communicate with consistent messages that adapt to different stages of the buying cycle. The process of managing sales opportunities with joined-up marketing recognises the role and relative importance of different influencers and decision makers and changes campaign emphasis depending on their views and concerns, objectives and interests.

Identify decision makers

In business purchasing, more than one person influences the choice of supplier. Individuals make different contributions to the decision-making process and they have different information requirements. Many companies have adopted team purchasing structures to deal with high value purchases and it is vital that you communicate effectively with every member of the team. Depending on the value and complexity of the purchase, a decision-making team could include:

- Senior executives.
- Purchasing professionals.
- Technical staff.
- Manufacturing managers.
- Service providers.
- Marketing staff.
- Departmental managers.

brilliant tip

Constant research is essential to ensure that your sales team is focusing on the right people at the right time. Purchasing situations are fluid and it would be easy to concentrate on the wrong members.

Build the right relationships

To drive the sale towards a conclusion you need to develop a programme that successfully builds relationships before, during and after the sale, qualifying the process all the way through. If the process works properly, the final negotiations are more of a formality than a pitch to secure a sale. The decision has often already been made. The initial contact, the proposal, visits to the website, meetings and discussions, presentations and support material have all contributed to a sales process where the decision makers recognise the value of your company over competitive offers.

Manage customer relationships

The traditional sales team focus is on short-term sales success. Moving to an account management process can help to build the broader focus that is essential to managing more complex sales opportunities. Building the essential broad customer relationships is a time-consuming process and that can pose problems for sales people who are used to improving sales productivity – achieving the highest levels of turnover for the minimum investment of time. Meeting other decision makers, reviewing progress on technical projects, making proactive customer care visits, arranging meetings between different members of the account team and briefing other specialists within the company – a traditional sales person would regard these as distractions from the main task of selling. It is vital that the sales people understand the importance of these activities and do not regard them as a waste of time.

Build understanding among all decision makers

Just getting the right message to the right person isn't enough. The aim is to ensure that, at every contact point, your communications build understanding among all decision makers.

When the decision makers are working as a team in your favour, your chances of success are high. Each decision maker will have their own agenda, but you should be encouraging a collaborative decision-making process that recognises your wider contribution to customer success.

brilliant impact

So, when a chief executive asks a technical director for an evaluation of your product, or discusses the potential financial benefits with the finance director, you can be confident that they will be basing their views on the information you have given them. What you are doing is creating a group of advocates within a customer organisation who share the same perception of your company and your products.

Nurture sales leads

Lead nurturing increases the value of your sales leads and enquiries to generate more revenue. A large proportion of early-stage leads that are poorly managed often end up lost, ignored or discarded. Too much time and money is spent on generating leads only to have them neglected. Lead management is the process that consolidates leads and enquiries from all sources, then qualifies, nurtures and converts them into sales-ready leads.

The key is to keep in touch, maintaining interest and providing the information that decision makers need. This takes a well-defined process to nurture your early-stage leads and build relationships before the buying process. Content is important here, so aim to keep in contact via:

> the key is to keep in touch

- Email.
- Newsletter.
- Case studies, reference sites and customer reviews on website.
- White papers.
- Conferences, workshops and webinars.
- Telephone.

Take an integrated approach

Bringing sales and marketing closer together is a means of accelerating the sales cycle and delivering exceptional results. The basis of the approach is to gather and share better customer and market intelligence through research and feedback and to use that data to win more customers. The improved understanding of customer issues and challenges makes it easier to create relevant, targeted communications with prospects throughout the sales cycle.

> bringing sales and marketing closer together is a means of accelerating the sales cycle and delivering exceptional results

It improves the results from sales and marketing activities by prioritising opportunities, maintaining the momentum of customer acquisition and speeding up the whole sales process. It also makes sales and marketing activities more accountable by measuring the results of campaigns against target revenues and numbers of closed customers.

Focus on the right prospects

In many business-to-business sectors, the sales and marketing environment is growing increasingly complex. In a typical scenario there may be 6–9 key decision makers and a sales process that could last 12–18 months from initial contact to closure. To maintain momentum, it's essential to communicate regularly and effectively with all prospects throughout the process. That requires ongoing research and collaboration between sales and marketing to gain a better understanding of the concerns and information needs of different decision makers. By working together and understanding the needs of the sales process, marketing can drive a bigger impact on sales by matching marketing communications to the time that is right for the sales process.

Gather intelligence

Changing roles, responsibilities and priorities within a decision-making group can impact on the success of a sales and marketing programme, so it is essential to maintain up-to-date information on key prospects. By continually gathering intelligence, sales and marketing teams can improve their understanding of prospects, their objections and any other barriers to a sale. The information will also help to build clearer sales profiles as a basis for focusing sales effort on the most appropriate prospects.

This requires an intelligence plan that gathers and builds essential insight throughout the sales and marketing process, covering key prospect data such as:

- Prospects' challenges.
- Prospects' objectives and goals.
- Levels of prospect awareness.
- Competitor information.

Use intelligent communications

The key to success is using intelligence to fine-tune communications. This can ultimately lead to a capability to personalise messages for each key prospect. By obtaining regular feedback, organisations can also identify a prospect's propensity to buy at different stages of the sales process. Communications can then be modified, with messaging refocused to reflect individual interests and concerns. This, in turn, will provide essential support to the direct sales effort and help to convert more prospects to customers.

Operate a marketing wave

When your company is planning marketing strategy, it's important to relate individual sales and marketing activities to overall strategies. A marketing wave is an integrated go-to-market plan that links sales strategies with lead generation, advertising and other marketing activities. In some cases, marketing waves can cross product and organisational boundaries with local campaign variations to ensure overall success.

A marketing wave describes the integrated strategy you develop to connect with your customers and the processes you use to manage customer interactions from initial contact through to order fulfilment. The process covers:

- Commercial strategy, objectives, and goals.
- Commercial execution across marketing, sales, pricing, and customer insight.
- Go-to-market capabilities, including organisation and process.

Marketing waves are designed to achieve measurable results and contribute to your company's strategic goals for revenue growth. They bring together all the assets that are essential to achieving those objectives in a single integrated plan.

Develop a marketing wave approach

A marketing wave enables your company to deliver its unique value proposition to the target market. The marketing wave identifies who your company will target, what it will offer customers, and how that will happen. A marketing wave takes into account the following factors:

● Market demand – what is driving or inhibiting market demand for your company's products?

● Customers – what are the customers' needs and challenges and what are their key decision-making factors?

● Competition – who are your main competitors and how well are they performing?

● Differentiation – what differentiators do you have? Are they sustainable and difficult to replicate by competitors?

● Solutions – what solutions best meet market demand and customer needs?

● Channels – what channel structure enables you to reach your target market cost effectively?

Take an integrated approach

A marketing wave brings together all the commercial functions – sales, marketing, brand management, pricing, and customer insight – into an integrated strategy that is aligned with business objectives and focused on profit.

brilliant impact

A marketing wave approach provides a number of important benefits:

● Ensures that your go-to-market strategy fits the current needs of your business objectives, channels and customers.

● Improves alignment and integration across the various commercial functions.

- Supports cost-reduction efforts without harming the core business.
- Brings together the right processes, people, and infrastructure to support an effective go-to-market strategy.
- Improves existing marketing and sales capabilities and helps you increase competitive advantage.
- Positions your company for sustained marketing improvement.

Clarify roles and responsibilities

When sales and marketing campaigns are managed on an ad hoc basis, responsibilities are poorly defined, and the result is tactical go-to-market plans and constant, disruptive requests for sales support. With integrated marketing waves, your sales and marketing teams can optimise their resources and deliver more effective results by collaborating throughout the sales cycle and focusing on the same business and strategic goals.

Focus on decision makers' real needs

Marketing waves can help companies move from a product-led sales and marketing operation to one that is focused on customers' business, technical and financial needs. Marketing waves start by building an understanding of the issues and challenges facing all members of the decision-making team and developing targeted communications and marketing campaigns that address those needs and move prospects towards a purchase decision.

Build a structured campaign

Marketing waves bring together disconnected sales and marketing activities, creating a structured campaign that contributes to your overall corporate goal. They bring together sales and marketing assets in a plan that is designed to achieve measurable results. This enables you to build a strong business case for the campaign, set the right budget and justify the marketing investment. Marketing waves contribute to your company's strategic goals for revenue growth, positioning awareness and customer retention by focusing on the campaigns that have the highest probability of contributing to measurable improvements in both short- and long-term goals.

Align sales and marketing operations

By integrating marketing waves, you can help both direct and indirect sales channels to succeed without providing ad hoc support for individual deals. Marketing waves incorporate elements to move your prospects through every stage of the sales process, from lead generation to completion. That can improve sales force productivity as well as make more efficient use of your marketing resources. In most companies, the individual sales and marketing programmes are likely to be in place. Using a marketing wave approach brings those elements together in an integrated strategy that delivers improved results.

Create clearly defined waves

Marketing waves should have a specific purpose within your overall business and marketing strategy. In the example that follows, the company's overall objective is to strengthen relationships with its customers by marketing a series of high value services that will increase customer dependency. The company develops a series of marketing waves that move the customer through the initial introduction of its services to a situation where the company is managing all of its customer's strategic services. Their aim is to demonstrate how attractive their service value proposition is to the customer. The waves consist of a pre-planned set of offerings that begin with an entry offering followed by other waves that create demand for other service offerings. Together, the waves provide a framework for building a pre-planned, structured approach that communicates the complete value proposition offered by your company.

example

To launch the services, the company operated four specific marketing waves:

1 Entry offer – to create interest and awareness of the service offer.
2 Assessment – to encourage customers to request an assessment to show how the service can deliver benefits.
3 Pilot project – to demonstrate the results of the service.
4 Managed service offer – to encourage customers to take the full service package.

1 Entry offer wave

To stimulate initial interest, the company focused its efforts on business decision makers, communicating potential benefits in business terms, not technology terms. The communications highlighted a key business problem and encouraged the prospect to take action by requesting white papers, subscribing to executive briefings, seminars and other information sources. To add value and credibility to the entry offer, the company used an independent authority to deliver the key messages. The aim of this wave was to demonstrate that the company understood the key challenges facing its customers and had the capability to deliver a solution to those challenges.

2 Assessment wave

At this stage, the company wanted to secure appointments to carry out assessments with those prospects that had requested initial information. As well as carrying out the assessment, the company used case studies and customer referral sites to provide proof that its services could deliver business and operational benefit. The company worked with prospects to put together a business case for the service, using input from the case studies.

3 Pilot project wave

In this wave, the company focused on organising a pilot project and helping prospects to assess the results from the project. The pilot project helped the company to lay the foundations for introducing an additional range of services. By demonstrating value in the pilot project, the company was able to upsell other services and increase its influence with the customer.

4 Managed services wave

The final wave was designed to build long-term dependent relationships with customers by offering them managed services – a solution where the service provider takes responsibility for running the customer's service-related activities and acts as a strategic partner.

Marketing plan in brief

Current situation

- Long gap between sales lead and purchase.
- Strengths of established sales processes and marketing campaigns.
- Weakness of lack of integration between sales and marketing.
- Threat of losing business opportunities.
- Opportunity to improve lead conversions.

Market requirements

- Customers looking for purchasing efficiencies.

Objectives

- Improve time to revenue.
- Improve return on marketing investment.

- Reduce competitive threats.
- Increase customer retention.

Strategy

- Research customers' purchasing process.
- Strengthen customer relationships.
- Integrate sales and marketing activities.
- Nurture sales leads to reduce time to purchase.
- Operate marketing waves to improve campaign focus.

Financial requirements

- Alignment of sales and marketing budgets to prioritise sales opportunities.

Communications

- Improve communications between sales and marketing teams.

Metrics

- Increased incremental revenue.
- Stronger business relationships at each stage.
- Higher value sales.
- Reduced sales costs.
- More profitable operations.

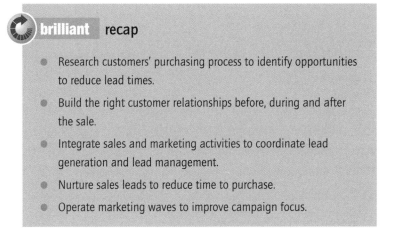

brilliant recap

- Research customers' purchasing process to identify opportunities to reduce lead times.
- Build the right customer relationships before, during and after the sale.
- Integrate sales and marketing activities to coordinate lead generation and lead management.
- Nurture sales leads to reduce time to purchase.
- Operate marketing waves to improve campaign focus.

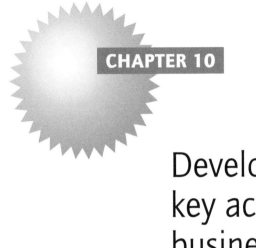

CHAPTER 10

Develop key account business

ntroducing key account management can benefit your business by increasing account control and improving the relationships between you and your most important customers. The closer working relationships enable you to plan the future development of your business with greater confidence and contribute to an overall reduction of your sales and supply costs.

Key account management and marketing strategy

Key account management contributes to the achievement of many aspects of your marketing strategy, including:

- Increase account control.
- Strengthen long-term customer relationships.
- Improve customer focus.
- Influence purchasing patterns.
- Create opportunities for repeat business.
- Control sales costs.
- Focus product planning.
- Improve long-term business performance.

Increase account control

> ### brilliant definition
>
> **Key accounts**
>
> Key accounts are the small group of large accounts that together make up the biggest proportion of a company's customer base. You need to protect those accounts because any loss could have a damaging effect on revenue and profit. The loss of a smaller account would not pose such a risk.

In business-to-business marketing, strong account relationships make an important contribution to long-term success. Key account programmes give you the opportunity to contact customers at regular intervals and build relationships that maintain the right level of control. This contact and control is important because it keeps key staff close to the customer, ensuring that they are aware of any competitive activity and helping to keep them up to date with the customers' changing business requirements. The regular contact available through the key account team also provides the opportunity to demonstrate customer care and take a proactive approach to customer relationships.

Strengthen long-term customer relationships

unless you understand the factors behind your success you cannot plan a customer retention strategy

Long-term customers add vital stability to a company. Most companies have a base of regular customers, but few know why those customers keep coming back. Quality, price, delivery, convenience; these are some of the factors that could explain why a customer continues to buy from your company, but unless you understand the factors behind your success you cannot plan a customer retention strategy for the future. You need to understand your customers' business, their plans, their key concerns and their views of you as a supplier, and you need to be certain that you can continue to provide them with the service they need.

brilliant impact

Long-term relationships are crucial to this process; by working closely with your customers, you can build an atmosphere of trust and confidence and ensure that any problems can be resolved without damaging the relationship.

Avoid price competition

brilliant example

A company supplying petrol charge cards to fleet operators faced the problem of annual contract negotiations with major customers who represented a high proportion of their turnover and profitability. The negotiations had traditionally been based on price, i.e. the cost of managing the fuel cards on behalf of the fleet operator, rather than quality of service. This made the charge card company vulnerable to aggressive pricing by competitors keen to win particular accounts.

However, research showed that fleet operators faced increasing administration costs in controlling overall fleet expenditure. By integrating their information systems with those of their key customers and developing tailor-made reporting systems, the charge card company was able to demonstrate a potential reduction in overall costs. The proposals on information systems enabled them to get involved in higher-level strategic discussions with fleet operators' senior management teams and demonstrate the benefits of a closer working relationship. These developments in administration helped to move the focus of the contract negotiations away from price to overall business benefits. The fleet operators were able to see the benefits of further enhancing the reporting procedures, and this provided the basis for long-term relationships which benefited both parties. The charge card company was able to retain business despite price competition, while the fleet operators improved efficiency and reduced overall costs.

Improve customer focus

Key account management involves many different departments within an organisation and this can help to focus attention on the needs of the customer. Effective key account management depends on a quality service from all staff and this can benefit your whole business.

brilliant example

When an international computer company wanted to build partnership with its key customers, it realised the importance of customer care, so it put its entire staff through a customer care training programme. This was a training programme on a large scale involving thousands of staff over a period of nearly a year. The company also developed a range of automated service and diagnostic tools to free staff so that they could spend more time on customer service.

Increased customer focus will benefit your business in a number of ways:

● Key account management will bring more of your staff into regular contact with customers, increasing levels of customer awareness and customer focus.

- Ensures that your staff are aware of their relationship to the customer and the contribution they can make to customer satisfaction.
- Builds team spirit and ensures that departmental objectives are integrated with corporate objectives.
- Provides a focal point for customer care training.
- Improves understanding of customer needs.
- Enables you to target key staff to get highest performance from staff with the greatest contribution to key account management.
- Ensures that your recognition and award schemes are encouraging long-term customer satisfaction.

Build company-wide customer focus

Customer focus is essential at all levels in the organisation. Although incentive and motivation schemes are used successfully in direct sales, their goals have usually been short term. A programme which encourages people to achieve higher levels of customer satisfaction must be long term and involve everyone who affects the

> customer focus is essential at all levels in the organisation

success of key account management. At senior management level, the programme must relate to overall performance so that managers focus on all the most important tasks that affect customer satisfaction. The senior manager programmes are cumulative, aiming at continuous improvement over a period of time. A scheme based on customer survey results provides a basis for rating different departments. The managers achieving the best ratings over a period of time are given a special award.

Employee programmes are used to motivate different groups and target key account staff. High visibility programmes involving the whole company are ideal for focusing attention on the general issues of key account management, but people need to be kept up to date.

Create team spirit

Key account management also raises customer awareness through its 'team' ethos. A group of European components manufacturers set up multi-disciplinary teams to help each other achieve best practice in areas critical to success. When one of the groups opened a new plant, the team worked together for a period of time to help the partner formulate a plan that would take advantage of the developments in other plants and utilise common resources. The result was that the new plant reflected the combined knowledge of the partners, and staff in each of the plants were more aware of each other's needs.

Influence purchasing patterns

Key account management can change the frequency of purchase cycles because of the higher levels of contact and the introduction of customer support services. In the capital goods business, for example, purchasing frequency might have been five years or longer, with little opportunity for contact and influence between major purchases. The next purchase was essentially a new buying situation. Key account management can shorten that cycle by focusing on the customer's needs through the life cycle of a product.

Analyse product life cycles

Every product goes through a life cycle and this can give important clues to the additional products and services a customer might need. Customers' needs change as they progress through the life cycle. They may need help in introducing a product, making the best use of it or preparing for change.

Life cycle analysis can be used in any purchase situation where frequency of contact is important. In the consultancy business, for example, key account management provides an opportunity to extend services upwards and downwards to change the frequency of purchasing. A design consultancy specialising in retail interiors can change its purchasing frequency by offering clients strategic retail consultancy at the top end and implementation services at the lower end. These services provide greater frequency of contact than the consultancy's basic design services. A management consultancy offering strategic business consultancy can support its customers and change purchasing cycles by offering training and project management services.

Create opportunities for repeat business

Key account management not only changes purchasing frequency, it can also open new sales channels. Key account management concentrates on repeat purchase and provides a valuable opportunity for selling additional products and services. For example, companies that market capital goods have an immediate opportunity to sell parts, service and accessories over an extended period, as well as a wide range of customer support services. If they develop their product range, they will find it easier to sell new products to partners.

brilliant tip

Key account management offers an opportunity to build customers for life.

Meet changing customer needs

Taking business banking as an example, the banks hold comprehensive information on their customers. Customers rarely change bank accounts, but their financial requirements change over a period of time – an ideal opportunity for meeting changing customer needs. The range of services to small businesses could include:

- Overdrafts.
- Payment services.
- Deposit services.
- Insurance.
- Start-up loans.

As the business grows, the range of services could change to include:

- Business development loans.
- Factoring.
- Leasing, contract hire and lease purchase.
- Investment finance.
- Electronic banking.
- Treasury services.
- International financial services.

However, unless the banks treat their customers as customers for life and look at their business with a degree of continuity, they will lose the incremental business opportunities to other financial institutions.

By giving customers access to electronic banking technology, for example, banks can provide key accounts with processes and systems that help them develop a competitive edge. Customers gain access to the bank's international networks and systems for carrying out transactions and processing information, and they do not have to invest in their own network. To help customers benefit from electronic banking, banks analyse the skills and training requirements, helping them to install any necessary equipment and familiarising staff with the new procedures. Because new users may not be familiar with the systems, the banks offer an advice and guidance helpline to reassure customers that they are fully supported.

The next stage is to show customers how to make the best use of electronic banking to improve their competitive edge. Here, the bank uses its experience of working with other businesses to provide a consultancy service to customers. As customers realign their business strategies to take advantage of the electronic banking network, they become increasingly dependent on a continuing relationship with the bank. As well as handling banking transactions, the banks can also offer their customers the use of the network for routine transactions. For example, a company with branch offices around the country can use the data network to communicate sales and financial information between branches and head office. The data network can also be used by customers to set up an interchange network with retailers to handle credit card authorisation, accounting, pricing, and other forms of settlement. This helps the company to achieve greater efficiency without investing in a network or the skills to manage it. It also opens up additional sales channels and enables the bank to introduce new revenue-earning services into the account.

Control sales costs

The cost of winning new business can be high, involving research, prospecting, progress meetings, proposals and development costs as well as the administrative costs of opening new accounts and setting up procedures to handle the work. Key account management is a powerful tool that locks suppliers and customers together into a mutually beneficial, stable relationship.

Key account management works on the basis that there is a cost and a degree of risk in replacing a supplier. Because customers are reluctant to change, or find there are considerable barriers to change, this can help to reduce your company's sales and mar-

> the emphasis is on providing a high quality, reliable service rather than on developing new leads

keting costs. The emphasis is on providing a high quality, reliable service rather than on developing new leads. Sales staff can concentrate on account development tasks and managing the teams of people who will provide support to the customer.

Focus product planning

Key account management allows you to find out more about your customers' needs and future plans. That, in turn, enables you to plan your own product developments in line with those needs. Understanding your customers' needs helps you to deal with issues such as:

- What direction should new product development take?
- What is the likely timetable for new product development?
- Have I got the skills and resources to meet future new product requirements?
- What are our customers' new product plans and how can we contribute to those?
- Can we help our customers develop new products that they would not otherwise be capable of?

In theory, product development programmes should not proceed without considerable investment in market research, but key account management will give a far more reliable insight into customer needs and provide a strong basis for development.

Involve customers in product launch

A transaction processing company which specialised in credit card processing had a small number of key customers among banks and other credit card issuers. As part of the account development process, the company operated a planned programme of new product releases – features or developments which the card issuers could incorporate into their own product development programmes. The plan was based on a quarterly release programme, that is, the new products were released on specific dates each year. However, customers were given advance notice of future releases so that they could consult the processing company and request modifications to the release programme for their own requirements. The release and consultation programme enabled the processing company to fine-tune its new product programme to reflect the precise requirements of its customers.

Encourage customer feedback

Although you may not be able to set up a formal process of consultation like the one just described, you can use the feedback processes that are built into key account management to evaluate your products and services. Participating in user groups or cooperating on joint development projects with your customers can also provide useful information on their design direction. An increasing number of companies are issuing a statement of direction which outlines how their business will develop over the medium and long term. By analysing the statement of direction and working out its implications for product development, you can align your own product development with that of your customers.

Improve long-term business performance

Building long-term relationships with customers is the basis for improving overall business performance.

- Key account management enables you to develop a long-term strategy that is based on a clear understanding of your customers' long-term needs.

- You can implement the strategy confident that you know who your customers will be in three to five years and confident that you can predict their levels of business.

- You can make product development and investment decisions confident that you have reduced the risk in the decision-making process.

- You can reduce costs by implementing continuous improvement processes that are based on an understanding of your customers' long-term needs.

- You should be able to increase levels of business without a corresponding rise in the cost of sales.

- You can reduce your skills development costs by investing in training that is geared to your customers' long-term needs.

The overall benefit of key account management is that it reduces the risk in planning and implementing a long-term business strategy and enables you to take actions that will improve overall performance.

brilliant example

A computer services division of an international information systems group wanted to improve its long-term performance by building closer relationships with its clients. Its traditional business of computer maintenance was being eroded by low-price competition from independent maintenance companies and those competitors were beginning to threaten other areas of the business. The division decided that it would only be able to compete effectively and maintain long-term turnover and profitability through key account management.

Key account management would enable the division to invest in new service tools and communications systems that would reduce the risk from price-based competitors. They would gain a better understanding of customers' long-term business plans and would be able to increase their range of services in line with customers' business plans. Key account management would also increase the level and quality of contact with customers and enable the division to communicate at a higher level to position itself as a strategic supplier. Over a three-year period, the division improved turnover and profitability to the point where it became the top-performing division in the group.

Marketing plan in brief

Current situation

- Company has a customer base of small and large accounts managed by the same sales force.
- Strengths of existing customer relationships.
- Weakness of poor account control at major customers.
- Threat of major revenue impact of major customer loss.
- Opportunity to minimise risk of major customer loss.

Market requirements

- Customers looking for close working relationships to gain business and technical benefits from suppliers.

Objectives

- Increase account control.
- Increase revenue.
- Control sales costs.
- Improve long-term business performance.

Strategy

- Strengthen long-term customer relationships.
- Improve internal customer focus.
- Influence customer purchasing patterns.
- Build repeat business levels.
- Focus product planning on customer needs.

Financial requirements

- Budget for communications programme.

Communications

- Develop communications programme for key account customers.
- Internal communications with account management team.

Metrics

- Increase in sales, revenue or profit by individual account.
- Reduction in customer churn.
- Reduction in sales costs.
- Customer satisfaction levels.

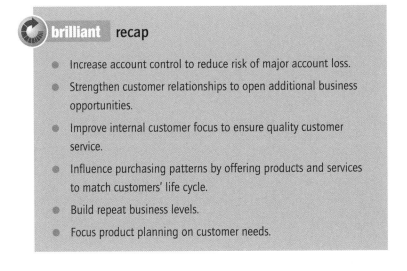

brilliant recap

- Increase account control to reduce risk of major account loss.
- Strengthen customer relationships to open additional business opportunities.
- Improve internal customer focus to ensure quality customer service.
- Influence purchasing patterns by offering products and services to match customers' life cycle.
- Build repeat business levels.
- Focus product planning on customer needs.

CHAPTER 11

Manage customer partnerships effectively

Partnership with major customers goes beyond key account management, involving more complex relationships and a longer-term commitment of resources. Partnership offers many business benefits; it also offers a high level of risk. Your senior management team should be closely involved in the decision-making process and should include executives responsible for finance, corporate planning, human resources and production, as well as marketing. In a smaller organisation, those functions may be combined, but it is essential that the strategic partnership decisions are made by the people who run the company.

Partnership and marketing strategy

Partnership can help to meet many different aspects of your marketing strategy. These are some examples:

- Increase sales to existing customers.
- Strengthen relationships with customers.
- Protect revenue streams.
- Counter competitive activity.

Manage partnership from the top

it is vital that
partnership is driven
from the top

It is vital that partnership is driven from the top because, without top-level commitment, it is difficult for a marketing executive to take the fundamental decisions that may be needed to transform the culture of an organisation. Partnership often has champions within an organisation – marketing or sales staff who can see the business benefits of developing closer relationships with customers – but they may not have the authority to take all the decisions that are necessary.

Partnership requires vision and strong leadership because the champion is committing a company to a course of action which can impact on its prospects for many years ahead. Setting up a partnership is not like opening an account for a new customer; it means aligning your business objectives with those of your customer and focusing on that relationship to the possible exclusion of other business opportunities. Partnership decisions are not to be taken lightly. The key management tasks include:

- Making strategic decisions to commit your company to partnership.
- Setting standards and introducing quality processes.
- Transforming the culture of the organisation.
- Building high-level relationships with partners.
- Investing in new products and services.

Take the strategic decisions

Your management team should be able to analyse the potential benefits of partnership and, conversely, the risks of not developing partnership. If your customers are determined to pursue partnership and reduce the number of suppliers, do you run the

definition

The main reasons for setting up partnerships include:

- Ensuring continuity of business in competitive markets.
- Providing a better basis for future planning.
- Ensuring access to growing markets.

risk of being excluded from some of the most important markets? Are your competitors likely to gain ground by building closer relationships if you reject an offer of partnership? Could the customers who want to pursue partnership take a more drastic course of action – merger or takeover for example – which may not be in the best interests of your company? If your partner's future plans include products for which your company is ideally suited, are you likely to lose future growth opportunities? If your potential partner dominates a market sector, are you likely to lose access to that market? What sort of risk does that pose?

Plan for change

dos and don'ts

These are the risks you must assess if you do not pursue partnership with an important customer, or if you reject the partnership offer by a dominant customer. These must be weighed carefully against the potential gains of partnership, and then reviewed again to assess the risks in meeting the requirements of partnership. Partnership will change your organisation and you need to be certain that you can meet the challenges and the costs of change.

These are some of the fundamental questions you should ask:

- What changes will be required to meet the short- and long-term requirements of partnership?
- How will other customers react to partnership with one important customer?
- Do the partnership benefits outweigh any potential loss of business from customers who might defect to competitors?
- Are your quality processes sufficient to meet your partner's requirements?
- What would be the cost and implications of upgrading those quality standards?
- Are current skills and staffing levels sufficient to meet the potential demands of partnership?
- What would be the cost of recruiting and developing new skills?
- Do you have the management skills to meet the changing requirements of partnership?
- Could your current management team grow into their new role through training and personal development, or would you have to recruit and build a new management team?
- What are the financial implications of partnership in terms of additional working capital or new investment to increase capacity or improve quality?
- Do you have access to those additional funds or would any change put a strain on your resources?
- If you need to expand your capacity, do you have room to grow or would you need to relocate? What impact would that have on your business?
- Given that the development of partnership will take up a great deal of senior management time and effort, can you commit your executive team to partnership, or will it divert them from other strategically important tasks?

- By developing partnership with one particular customer, are you putting up barriers to important business opportunities with other key customers?

There are likely to be many other factors specific to your industry or specific to a particular partner which must be considered, but these are questions that every company must consider because they impact on both day-to-day activities and the long-term development of the business. Before committing your organisation to partnership, you must be sure that you have made the right decision. A partnership that benefits your customers but locks you into a cycle of increased costs and distracts you from your long-term goals is a one-way partnership and may not be in your best interests.

Commit resources to partnership

If you decide that the benefits of partnership outweigh the risks, you must commit your whole organisation to partnership. This means committing time to set up and operate the partnership, committing people and developing their skills and committing funds to investing in new levels of service. This commitment does not suddenly begin when the partnership starts to operate; there is a considerable commitment in planning the partnership and deciding how it will operate. There are two distinct phases:

> commitment does not suddenly begin when the partnership starts to operate

- Getting the commitment of all your people and selecting and developing the team to drive partnership forward.
- Introducing partnership to your customers and demonstrating your capability to potential partners.

You and your senior executive team must decide whether you will be involved throughout the process or whether you will delegate tasks to other members of staff, and you must determine the level of resources you will commit to each stage.

Commit people

In this phase, you will be changing attitudes within the organisation, developing skills and establishing the processes that will be needed for partnership. You will have to commit time and resources in a number of different areas:

- Setting the overall direction for change and providing input to the corporate plan.
- Developing a mission statement and achieving the commitment of all staff to the mission.
- Developing the guidelines for an internal communications programme and allocating funds to the programme.
- Establishing the skills requirements and allocating a budget for customer service training.
- Selecting and appointing the team which will drive the partnership programme forward and allocating funds to the key tasks they identify.

Demonstrate capability

This stage involves a major investment in communications – both personal communications at many different levels within the potential partner's organisation, and individual communications to reach the contacts that are not easily accessible. Your key tasks at this stage are to manage perceptions of your organisation and change attitudes within potential partner companies, and to achieve these you will have to commit people and support them with communications budgets. The important tasks would include:

- Conducting strategic discussions with senior executives of the partner companies.

- Allocating funding to seminars and management briefings and appointing members of the partnership team to participate in these events.
- Allocating funds to documentation and other support activities during the negotiations.
- Developing a communications strategy and allocating funds to the operation of the communications programme.

Many of the tasks in this phase will involve the work of specialists within the partnership team. Your role will be to set the overall direction, maintain the impetus of the programme and build effective relationships with your partner's senior management team.

Transform the culture of the organisation

Effective performance depends not just on the actions of a few individuals, but on the total commitment of everyone in the organisation.

brilliant example

In a manufacturing company, for example, some of the processes critical to the success of partnership are carried out by people who do not see their jobs as customer-focused – invoice clerks, delivery drivers, maintenance engineers, telephone receptionists, warehouse staff and development engineers. However, their role is crucial to the efficient day-to-day operation of partnership and, without their commitment and understanding, partnership is likely to fail.

There are a number of important tasks:

- Provide a vision of the way your company should operate and how your customers should see the company.

- Communicate the needs of partnership to everyone in your organisation.

- Present the vision in terms of tangible objectives for each department within the organisation.

- Formulate an action plan that will enable each department to achieve their objectives.

- Allocate the resources to achieve departmental objectives.

- Introduce a reporting mechanism that will enable the departments to communicate with each other and demonstrate overall corporate progress.

- Allocate resources to motivation and incentive programmes designed to improve organisational performance.

- Develop recognition schemes to reward improvement.

Communicate a vision

A mission statement sets the direction for everyone in the business. It shows that every manager and every employee is concerned with meeting customer needs, all of the time, whatever they do. The vision itself counts for nothing unless it is accompanied by action from the top. Senior executives who demonstrate a personal commitment to partnership by setting their own personal quality standards, taking part in customer meetings and participating in improvement programmes set an example for everyone in the organisation. By adopting a high profile, they can attract media attention and build awareness of the company's capability and commitment.

> the vision counts for nothing unless it is accompanied by action from the top

Build high-level relationships

While your partnership team is developing relationships at different levels within the customer organisation, you need to build a matching top-level commitment from your customer's senior executive team.

brilliant tip

Your potential partners face important decisions and risks, and they need your reassurance on certain key issues before they get deeply involved with you.

Although it is your sales people who will make the initial contact, they may not have the experience or the authority to discuss strategic business issues with a senior management team.

By getting involved in the negotiations, you show that partnership is important to your company and that you are prepared to put the full weight of your position behind the success of the partnership. Seminars and management briefings are important in helping senior executives to understand the benefits and implications of partnership for their organisation. By participating in this type of event, you are showing that partnership is a strategic issue which should be discussed at board level. You will also have the opportunity to provide a first-hand account of how you would deal with the executive team's concerns. Among the questions in the minds of your partner's executive team will be:

- Does your organisation have the capability to deliver a sustained quality of service over the long term?
- Does your organisation have the resources to grow in line with changing business requirements?

- Is your organisation flexible enough to respond to changing business and market requirements?
- How important is partnership to your organisation and how would you demonstrate your commitment to success?
- Will the partners have access to your senior management team and what escalation procedures will be in place in the event of any problem?

By helping senior executives to make decisions about partnership, you can ensure that negotiations are conducted at the right level and that partnership will be properly evaluated.

Introduce new products and services

As part of the development of partnership, you may want to introduce new products and services so that your range is closely aligned to the needs of your partners. New product development can involve high levels of risk, so it is important that any decisions are made at senior level. You can find out more about new product development in Chapter 1.

- Will the new product or service evolve from your existing range?
- What is the likely development cost?
- Will the development programme interfere with other strategically important development projects?
- Will the new product provide you with competitive advantage in any other sectors?
- Does the new product development programme introduce risks of failure or potential damage to the partnership?
- If you do not develop the new product, will your competitors have an opportunity to regain lost ground with your partners?
- Can you take advantage of your partners' technology or development facilities to speed up the process of new product development?

Effective new product development will ensure that you maintain the momentum of the partnership, but the projects need to be carefully integrated with your corporate development programme to ensure that they do not affect your progress in other markets. Key actions to ensure the success of your new product programmes include:

- Setting priorities for new products.
- Allocating sufficient funds to new product development.
- Encouraging and rewarding innovation.
- Encouraging proactive research and development in line with your partners' objectives.

Marketing plan in brief

Current situation

- Company has a number of large accounts with which it has built dependent relationships.
- Strengths of established relationships and collaboration.
- Weakness of internal commitment to success of partnership.
- Threat of customer loss to competitors.
- Opportunity to increase account revenue and profitability.

Market requirements

- Customers want to gain increased business and technical benefits from partners.

Objectives

- Increase sales to existing customers.
- Strengthen relationships with customers.

- Protect revenue streams.
- Counter competitive activity.

Strategy

- Manage partnership relationships from the top.
- Commit company resources to partnership.
- Transform company culture to ensure quality service.
- Build high-level relationships with partners.
- Customise products and services for partners.

Financial requirements

- Budget for communications programme.

Communications

- Develop communications programme for partners.
- Internal communications with account management team.

Metrics

- Increase in sales, revenue or profit by individual account.
- Reduction in customer loss.
- Reduction in sales costs.
- Customer satisfaction levels.

brilliant recap

● Manage partnership relationships from the top to ensure commitment to success.

● Mobilise company resources to build successful partnership at all levels of collaboration.

● Transform company culture to ensure quality service.

● Build high-level relationships with partners to ensure understanding of the strategic benefits of partnership.

● Customise products and services for partners.

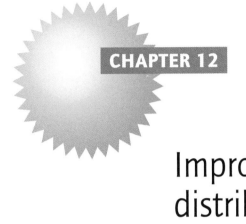

CHAPTER 12

Improve distributor performance

Distributors provide sales, marketing and customer service functions on behalf of manufacturers or suppliers. They act as agents or representatives, enabling manufacturers to reach geographically remote customers or niche market sectors that they could not support cost effectively using their own internal resources. Improving distributor performance helps companies to sell more products or enhance levels of service to their smaller customers.

Distributor performance and marketing strategy

Improving distributor performance can impact many different aspects of marketing strategy. These are some examples:

- Increase sales to smaller customers.
- Provide greater coverage.
- Improve after-sales support to customers.
- Enter new market sectors.

Set performance objectives

Increase sales to smaller customers

How important are distributors to your business? Do your distributors 'own' the relationship with your customers?

Distributors generally deal with a supplier's smaller customers, leaving your sales force to focus on key accounts. How can you influence distributors to improve sales to your smaller customers?

Provide greater coverage

Can your sales force provide the coverage you need to reach all your customers economically? If you sell products or services to a number of different market segments, you may not have the resources to develop your business in all segments. By working with distribution partners that have specialist knowledge of the segment, you can operate the equivalent of a niche marketing strategy.

Is lack of an international presence holding back your export plans? Working in partnership with distributors opens wider geographical markets. Setting up a dedicated global distribution network, for example, would require a massive investment of time and resources for one company. Using established networks of intermediaries that offer global coverage provides a rapid, low cost solution.

Improve after-sales support to customers

Is after-sales support important to your customers? Do you have to operate a field service team to support customers? Could a third-party service operation provide an alternative service solution? Distributors can provide an after-sales service to all of a manufacturer's customers, large and small, by holding stocks of spare parts and providing a local technical and maintenance service.

Enter new market sectors

Do you want to enter new market sectors, but face difficult barriers to entry? Do you lack the skills and knowledge to enter the target sector? Distributors make it easier for you to enter new markets. You can draw on the distributor's market penetration and knowledge rather than commit sales and marketing resources to build a presence from scratch. Distributors can also offer coverage and specialist knowledge of small niche markets that provide an additional outlet for low volume products in your range.

Identify development requirements

What form of support do distributors need to improve their performance? If you have a large distributor network, do you operate a tiered structure that recognises different levels of business and capability? There are four key steps:

- Research local market conditions.
- Set up a local market team.
- Share experience for success.
- Select the type of support.

Research local market conditions

Market research can help you to identify the factors that differentiate local markets. These might include:

- Economic prosperity.
- Market maturity.
- Competitive activity.
- Customer decision-making process.
- Distribution infrastructure.
- Quality of marketing services.
- Marketing media available.
- Awareness of your company.

Set up a local market team

You should set up a team to work with local distributors to help them develop their strategy and plan their programme of sales and marketing activities. The team would arrange regional meetings to help local distributors identify the right strategic marketing mix and messaging. To help them implement the programme, the team can recommend local approved marketing agencies that work within the framework of your overall marketing strategy and can ensure that local marketeers are up to date with the latest campaigns and creative strategies.

Share experience for success

Local markets share many common characteristics, as well as clear local differences. Sharing experience and best practice can help all local markets, so consider setting up a local market forum. The more mature markets may have case studies and proven campaigns to share, while younger territories can share their experiences. This experience can help to identify the support requirements for other territories or groups of distributors.

Select the type of support

---

brilliant impact

When distributors have the right level of market awareness and support, they can deliver added value and play a proactive role in marketing your products and services.

You can design programmes to help distributors grow their own business and make it easier for all parties to work together. A business education programme will help distributors keep up with the latest developments and maintain their product and business skills. Courses could cover management development, product marketing skills, industry knowledge, and sales and marketing tools.

> you can design programmes to make it easier for all parties to work together

Structure the channel

How do you structure your distributor channel? Should you have different levels of distributor? How can distributors move up the structure and what are the benefits? There are two key actions:

- Attract high quality distributors.
- Set up a tiered structure.

Attract high quality distributors

Your channel marketing programme should focus on attracting and supporting high calibre distributors so that they can deliver a high standard of service to your customers. Marketing support includes product and business development, training, product information, branding programmes and co-marketing activities.

Build a strong channel network by attracting distributors that have the technical capability and market coverage to serve your

brilliant example

The Cisco Channel Partner Program is a good example, offering distributors benefits such as certification for technical staff, access to market-leading products and services, marketing and financial support, and opportunities for business growth.

customers. Offer potential distributors the opportunity to participate in a structured programme.

Set up a tiered structure

Establish a tiered structure for your distributor network that provides partners with increasing levels of support as they achieve higher ranking. The Cisco Channel Partner Program, for example, offers different tools and resources to Registered, Authorised or Certified partners. Work with distributors to help them develop their business so that they can move up the structure and deliver increasingly higher standards of service.

Deliver a certification programme for distributor technical staff that develops essential skills in deploying and supporting your products. The programme can include distance learning programmes as well as practical, hands-on training workshops on your site or in educational institutes.

Deliver information

Availability of up-to-date business, technical and marketing information is essential to the operation and development of a distributor network. To ensure that information is used effectively, take three important actions:

- Keep distributors up to date.
- Develop accessible communications.
- Set up a portal system.

Keep distributors up to date

Effective communication throughout the distributor network helps improve the efficiency of your marketing operations.

Communication enables all members of the distribution network to share essential market and operational information so that they can respond quickly and effectively to changes in the marketplace. You should provide essential market information that helps distributors plan their own marketing and investment programmes. If you have acquired new customers, launched new products or entered new market sectors, the changes will have an impact throughout the distributor network.

brilliant tip

Regular marketing communications also build teamwork by keeping all parties informed on developments that affect their operations and by helping them to grow their own business. By bringing together all parties through communications, you can build an efficient, responsive network that operates as a single, coordinated unit.

Develop accessible communications

Providing a single integrated source of information creates a distributor network that can respond rapidly to change or new opportunities. The problem is that as the distributor network grows, the task of trying to communicate with members who might be located anywhere in the world over a variety of different communication networks, devices and standards gets more and more complex. The communication network should therefore be based on open standards so that all members can communicate regardless of the nature of their internal IT systems.

Set up a portal system

Set up information portals for distributors to strengthen relationships and improve productivity. The portal should include a document resource library, marketing collateral, e-learning tools, certification management tools and other important business development material. Incorporate a secure forum to allow distributors to share information and build a sense of community. Putting the material in a portal reduces distribution costs and ensures that material is available to the entire network. However, the onus is on individual distributors to access and use material, so it is important to monitor portal activity to measure how content is being used.

Provide marketing support

Marketing support is key to developing business through a distributor network. Support can take the form of training, provision of marketing materials or joint marketing initiatives. These are the important elements in a support plan:

- Incorporate mandatory programmes.
- Offer local outlets choice.
- Provide a marketing support guide.
- Localise marketing programmes.
- Support direct marketing.
- Run a customised advertising service.
- Supply advertising material.

Incorporate mandatory programmes

While customised support programmes have benefits for both you and your distributors, there are a number of programmes that are crucial to achieving the right standards of customer service. These programmes give you a degree of control over critical local operations. Training programmes which improve the quality of customer service should be an integral part of a distributor support programme. Although the courses and the method of delivery can be tailored to suit local markets and the local skills profile, participation must be mandatory to ensure that all distributors deliver a consistently high standard of service.

Offer local outlets choice

By offering local outlets a choice of programmes, you can tailor your marketing to suit local market conditions. The programmes might include:

- Local advertising.
- Direct mail.
- Product literature.
- Display material.
- Merchandising material.
- Special offers.
- Public relations support.

Provide a marketing support guide

You can produce a guide to support programmes which enables the local outlet to select programmes that allow them to develop their own promotional strategies. The guides should:

- Explain the scope and benefits of individual programmes.
- Describe the support material available to operate the programme.
- Explain how to order support material.
- Provide guidelines on running the programmes.

Localise marketing programmes

Because there are so many possible variables in different markets, you should develop localisation kits that will enable you to customise your creative work to incorporate the most relevant messaging, images, offers and creative treatment while retaining the value and strength of your brand. This approach gives you real creative and commercial flexibility.

The localisation process can be applied to:

- Email.
- Newsletters.
- Advertisements.
- Direct mail.
- Online activities.
- Publications.
- Customer magazines.

The key stages in localisation are analysing and refining messages to reflect levels of market maturity and awareness of local issues, and selecting appropriate images or graphics to suit the local culture.

Support direct marketing

The essence of an effective local support programme is that local distributors understand their customers' needs and communicate with messages tailored to that market. The most powerful medium to achieve that is direct marketing – a powerful weapon in the hands of local outlets because it enables them to talk to their customers on their own terms. The key to the success of local direct marketing programmes is detailed knowledge of the local customer base so that the offers and information can be tailored to local marketing programmes. The most efficient way to handle this is to maintain a central database of all local customers and use database management techniques to manage the mailing list. Local distributors are unlikely to have the sophisticated equipment needed to carry out database management operations and the exercise can be carried out more efficiently on a central database. Information for the database can be gathered from a number of sources, including:

- Local customer sales records.
- Replies to advertisements.
- Responses to special offers or invitations.
- Market research.

Run a customised advertising service

Local or regional advertising campaigns can be customised to suit the needs of the local market. Support can be delivered in a number of forms:

- Funds to enable local outlets to produce and run their own advertisements.
- Contributions to the cost of joint supplier/local outlet advertisements.
- Contributions to the cost of advertisements run by regional groups of outlets.
- Production of national support advertisements which incorporate local information and which are run on a regional basis.

The level of financial support depends on the funds available for local support and your local distributors' own budgets. For example, many independent outlets have substantial advertising budgets of their own and utilise the suppliers' budgets to supplement their own or to run specific campaigns. Other smaller outlets or franchised outlets without their own budgets rely entirely on the supplier's contribution to run local campaigns. Because of this, the question of financial support is usually subject to negotiation.

Supply advertising material

You can also supply support in the form of complete advertisements, logos, artwork or photographs for inclusion in the outlet's own local campaigns. As you are more likely to be concerned about the consistency of local advertisements than the local outlet, you should issue clear guidelines on the use of different elements of corporate identity. Many suppliers provide advertising standard manuals which give examples of layouts for different sizes of advertisements, explain the position and size of the company name and logo, list the typefaces to use and include sample advertisements for guidance.

Alternatively, you can offer local outlets a central advertising service. This support policy enables you to offer local outlets consistent professional advertisement standards, with local information such as name and address, map, priced offers, product variations and special offers incorporated. The local outlet benefits from national advertising and strong branding, but they have advertisements that suit the local market.

Marketing plan in brief

Current situation

- Distributor network serves smaller customers.
- Strengths of established network providing broad coverage.
- Weakness of variable sales performance and customer service standards across the network.

- Threat of competitive gains.

- Opportunity to increase sales and improve relationships with smaller customers.

Market requirements

- Smaller customers look for high standards of support and service from distributors.

Objectives

- Increase sales to smaller customers.

- Provide greater coverage.

- Improve after-sales support to customers.

- Enter new market sectors.

Strategy

- Set performance objectives.

- Identify development requirements.

- Structure the distributor network.

- Deliver business and market information.

- Provide marketing support.

Financial requirements

- Fund marketing support programme.

- Invest in distributor information system.

Communications

- Communicate benefits of joining distributor network.

- Communicate requirements of performance programme.

▶

Metrics

- Increase in sales, revenue or profit by individual outlet, distributor group or network.
- Increase in distributor sales to existing customers.
- Distributor sales to new customers.
- Gains from competitive accounts.
- Customer satisfaction levels.

brilliant recap

- Set performance objectives to improve the results distributors can achieve.
- Identify development requirements and create a plan.
- Structure the distributor network to give distributors an incentive to improve performance and enjoy higher levels of support.
- Deliver business and market information efficiently so that distributors can respond to business opportunities.
- Provide marketing support to help distributors achieve sales and marketing targets.

CHAPTER 13

Control
competitors

Are competitors threatening critical areas of your business? To counter and control competitive actions, you need to identify the advantages you and your competitors have over each other. By monitoring and analysing competitive activity, you can predict competitor behaviour – what they are planning and how they might react to moves that you make.

Competitive activity and marketing strategy

Controlling competitive activity can help to meet many different aspects of your marketing strategy. These are some examples:

- Maintain sales to existing customers.
- Protect revenue streams.
- Win business from new accounts.
- Counter competitive activity.

Identify the competitive threat

Competitor information helps you to identify how you can protect your most important business and, more positively, how you can strengthen your position with customers in situations where your competitors are currently holding a larger share of the business than you.

Competitor intelligence is freely available from the internet, the press and other published sources. Information from these sources can provide a valuable starting point for developing more detailed competitor profiles. These are the main questions you should be asking:

> competitor intelligence
> is freely available

- How many competitors do you have?
- Who are your major competitors?
- Are they direct or indirect competitors?
- Where are your main competitors located?
- How do they compare in size?
- What percentage of your business do they threaten?
- Which of your competitors has the strongest growth prospects?
- Which customers might defect to competitors?
- How strong are competitors' relationships with key decision makers?
- How have levels of business changed over the past three years?
- Are there any significant developments which have affected these changes?
- How long have they been dealing with key customers?
- How do your products compare with competitive offerings?
- What are your competitors' main strengths? How do prices compare? What are their standards of customer service?
- Have they invested in links with customers which would make it difficult for other suppliers to make inroads?
- Have you got the skills and resources to overcome the competitive threat?
- Are any competitors making inroads into businesses where you are currently the dominant supplier?

- What are customers' attitudes towards your competitors?
- How do they compare with attitudes towards your company?
- Who are your competitors main customers?
- Which of your competitors' customers do you want to win?

Compare key competitive factors

Listed below are a number of factors that are important to quality service. You can use these factors to compare how your company and your main competitors score on each of the factors. The results should be used as the basis for a programme of performance improvement.

- Degree of commitment to quality service.
- Level of staff understanding and awareness of customer service.
- How 'customer-focused' is the organisation.
- Existence of measurable service standards.
- Existence of suitable customer feedback mechanisms.
- Existence of suitable complaints management procedures.
- Degree of customer retention.
- Customer focus of product development processes.
- Commitment to quality service delivery.
- Scope of pre-sales activity.
- Simplicity of enquiry and ordering.
- Quality of product/service delivery.
- Efficiency of purchase administration.
- Effectiveness of sales follow-up.
- Quality of after-sales support.

Use the sales force

The sales force can obtain competitor information from many different sources. By talking to customers, they can find out about competitors' direct sales calls, direct marketing campaigns, special offers and new developments. They can also obtain similar information from retailers or distributors. The sales force may be able to provide a profile of your most important competitors.

Analyse published information

Information is readily available from publications, the press and the internet that can help you gather intelligence on different aspects of competitors' business, including:

● Main markets.

● Customers.

● Resources and financial performance.

● Product range.

● New products.

● Plans for growth.

Obtain competitor literature

Corporate brochures and annual reports are the best sources of published information. You can obtain copies from exhibitions, customers or as downloads from competitors' websites.

Monitor the press

Maintain a file of press cuttings on your competitors' activities using their trade publications as a source. You can use a press cutting agency to gather material for you. Ask them to provide you with any cuttings that include the names of your competitors.

Analyse industry reports

Published industry surveys can provide a useful insight into purchasing patterns in different marketing sectors. You can obtain information on competitors, market share and industry trends. Industry surveys are often sponsored by magazines, industry associations or groups of manufacturers.

Check the internet

Competitor websites can provide valuable information on their resources, plans and capabilities. As well as checking the company information and product pages, you should read any customer case studies on the site and monitor the news section to find out about new developments. The internet is also a valuable source of other competitor research material. Industry newsletters or summaries of published research could prove a valuable starting point. Trade publications are increasingly available in electronic editions, making it easier for you to monitor the press.

Visit exhibitions

Competitors' exhibition stands can be valuable sources of information. Most companies only participate in exhibitions that are important to their current or future business plans. Frequently, they choose to exhibit because they have a new product to announce.

Monitor competitors' marketing activities

Analysing competitor marketing strategies will help you to respond to their activities.

By monitoring competitor advertising, promotions, exhibition presence, press activities and internet information you can assess possible strategies. These are some of the possible scenarios:

- Heavy advertising expenditure could indicate a competitor trying to win greater share.

- Price promotions may indicate that your competitors want to be perceived as value-for-money suppliers.

- Press announcements about new production facilities could indicate that your competitors are trying to significantly increase their business.

- Announcements about new branch or dealership openings could mean that competitors are expanding into new territories.

Marketing publications can be useful sources of information on competitor marketing activity. They contain news of recent campaigns, league tables of expenditure by different companies and analysis of company strategies. The recruitment and appointments sections of marketing publications can also highlight changes in strategy.

Appoint a research company

If you do not have the internal resources to monitor competitive activity, you can use an independent research company to carry out all the tasks outlined above. You can also ask them to carry out research into customer attitudes to competitors. Customers may be more willing to provide this information to an independent organisation.

brilliant dos and don'ts

Proceed with caution

You should be cautious in acting on competitor intelligence. Published sources can only provide a partial picture; more strategic information is likely to be confidential. This means that you may make incorrect assumptions in planning your response to competitor action.

Take action

Competitor information is only valuable if you use it to refine your own strategies or take defensive action to protect your business. Simply gathering information without analysis or action is wasteful.

You know your products and your customers, but how do you know what marketing and communications will be effective? What makes your business unique? What is its competitive advantage? To market yourself successfully, it's essential to understand your competitive advantage – what differentiates you and makes you a more suitable supplier. The differentiators could be product performance, price, quality, capacity, delivery time or financial stability. The starting point is to identify your competitive advantages and to build those advantages into customer communications and marketing programmes.

Identify your competitive advantage

Sustainable competitive advantage is linked to an ability to innovate. Although investment in improvements to existing products and processes does bring growth, it is new, innovative breakthroughs that enable a company to take advantage of changing market conditions, supporting continued growth and creating a high return on investment.

> sustainable competitive advantage is linked to an ability to innovate

Before you can identify your own competitive advantage, you must understand your competitors. Competitive intelligence, described in the previous section, can be useful for marketing, pricing, managing and other aspects of strategic planning. The input from this research can be used for benchmarking your company against your competitors.

brilliant definition

Competitive advantage

There are two basic types of competitive advantage:

- Cost advantage.
- Differentiation advantage.

Cost advantage exists when a company can deliver the same benefits as competitors but at a lower cost. With differentiation advantage, the company delivers benefits that exceed those of its competitors. Companies with both types of competitive advantage can deliver superior value for customers and improved profits for the business.

brilliant example

Ryanair differentiated itself through low prices and the offer of a no-frills service to airline passengers. Dell established a new business model for the computer industry by selling online and offering buyers the opportunity to create their own customised product. Publishers Waterstones created a welcoming environment in its stores by encouraging people to relax and browse books. They differentiated the experience of dealing with the company.

Choose the right competitive strategy

You can adopt four generic business strategies to gain competitive advantage:

- Differentiation in a broad market.
- Cost leadership in a broad market.
- Differentiation focus on a niche market.
- Cost focus on a niche market.

Differentiation

A differentiation strategy involves focusing on specific criteria used by buyers in a market and positioning your company as uniquely qualified to meet those criteria. Typically, this type of product would carry a premium price that reflects the higher production costs, tighter quality processes and extra features provided for the customer. Communication is based on building customer preference for a superior brand and justifying the premium price. This type of strategy is suitable for products like luxury cars, high specification consumer electronics or 'gold standard' services such as premium bank accounts.

Cost leadership

Companies following this strategy aim to become the lowest-cost producer across all sectors of their chosen market. This strategy is common to large corporations that offer standard 'commodity products' with little differentiation and which appeal to large numbers of customers. Where price is perceived as an important factor by customers, a low-cost leader with a significant cost advantage over competitors is likely to achieve a large market share. This type of strategy is suitable for mass-market products like mid-range cars, retail chains and consumer durables.

Niche differentiation

With a niche differentiation strategy, a company aims to differentiate within small niche market segments where it can identify specific customer needs that are not met by the mass-market offerings of competitors. To succeed, it is essential to ensure that customers really do have different needs and wants, and that there are sufficient customers to support a profitable sales and marketing operation. This type of strategy is suitable for specialist retailers or organisations offering specialist services, such as educational travel.

Niche cost leadership

Companies following a niche cost leadership strategy concentrate on building a cost advantage in a small number of niche segments. Typically, they offer basic or lower specification versions of mass-market products and services that appeal to price-conscious buyers. This type of strategy is suitable for retailers and manufacturers who concentrate on discount or own-label products.

Make the most of your resources

Every company has a set of resources and capabilities that it can use to build a competitive advantage. The stronger those resources and capabilities compared to the competition, the bigger the advantage. However, where there is no real differentiation, competitors can easily replicate products and services, creating a commodity market where none of the players has any specific advantage. These are examples of resources that competitors would find it difficult to replicate easily:

> every company has a set of resources and capabilities that it can use to build a competitive advantage

- Patents and trademarks.
- Proprietary knowledge.
- Customer base.
- Corporate reputation.
- Brand equity.

However, as well as having resources, you must also have the capability to use them effectively and profitably. This is derived from business processes, quality procedures, organisational structures, corporate culture, recruitment and training processes, and relationships with suppliers and business partners.

Together, they give your company the capability to operate in a way that delivers success through innovation, efficiency, quality, and customer focus. These capabilities are intangible and can be even more difficult for competitors to replicate.

Focus on strengths

You can use your resources and capabilities either to lower your cost structure or to differentiate yourself through superior products. You can use either strategy to position yourself against competitors. You also need to decide whether to use your strengths across the whole of your chosen market or to focus on a specific sector where the combination of resources and capabilities gives you greatest advantage. That means a company that does not have the scale or resources to compete across the board can be extremely successful by concentrating on niche markets.

Use the resources of partners

You can improve competitive advantage by drawing on the resources of partners in your supply chain. The concept of a business ecosystem takes this to its logical conclusion by building a loose network of customers, manufacturers, suppliers, distributors, service providers, manufacturers of related products or services, technology providers, and other support organisations that rely on the strength of the network as a whole for their own success.

Member companies do not depend on their own internal capabilities for success: they can draw on the skills and resources of partners. Members aim to improve the overall health of their ecosystem by contributing to a set of common assets that other companies can use to improve their own competitive performance. This might take the form of communications tools to connect members, or knowledge and resources to speed up and simplify the development of new products by other members.

Build sustainable competitive advantage

Sustainable competitive advantage is vital to long-term survival and profitability. To achieve this, your company must be responsive to changing market and competitive conditions and innovative so that it can quickly develop new products and services to meet those changes.

brilliant tip

Competition on a global scale and the emergence of new forms of competition mean that you must be adaptable and able to change quickly to maintain competitive advantage.

Plan for business transformation

The pace and level of competition may become so fierce that it is necessary to transform the business. As an example, the development of information technologies has given smaller companies the ability to compete effectively with much larger organisations. In some markets, such as telecommunications, deregulation has broken up the monopolies of large organisations and given their smaller competitors new business opportunities. In this scenario, both large and small competitors may need to transform their business model to adapt and survive in the new marketplace. That means identifying new opportunities and strategies to build or protect competitive advantage, focusing on new product development, growing market share, strengthening customer loyalty and eliminating communication barriers.

Monitor longer-term changes

Long-term corporate success is linked to the ability to innovate. Although investment in improvements to existing products and processes does bring growth, it is the

> long-term corporate success is linked to the ability to innovate

ability to respond to changing customer needs and market conditions with innovative solutions that enables successful entry into new markets, rapid growth and a higher return on investment.

Marketing plan in brief

Current situation

- Competitors threatening customer base.
- Strengths of competitor awareness and own competitive advantage.
- Weakness of growing competitive threat.
- Threat of significant account loss.
- Opportunity to build sustainable competitive advantage.

Market requirements

- Customers looking for suppliers offering best quality and service.

Objectives

- Maintain sales to existing customers.
- Protect revenue streams.
- Win business from new accounts.
- Counter competitive activity.

Strategy

- Identify competitive threat.
- Monitor competitive activity.
- Assess competitive strengths.
- Build sustainable competitive advantage.

Financial requirements

- Investment in service standards and product quality to ensure competitive advantage.

Communications

- Customer communications to raise awareness of competitive advantage.

Metrics

- Reduction in customer losses.
- Increased market penetration against competitors.
- Gains at competitive accounts.

brilliant recap

- Identify competitive threat and compare competitors' performance and advantages.
- Monitor competitive activity, particularly on your own accounts.
- Assess your own competitive strengths.
- Build sustainable competitive advantage.

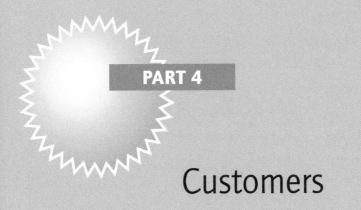

PART 4

Customers

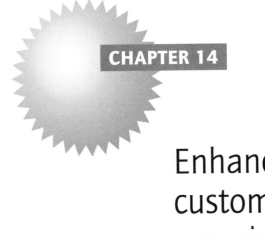

CHAPTER 14

Enhance the
customer
experience

mproving the customer experience infrastructure is good for business. In fact, research indicates that consumers would recommend a company that provided an outstanding customer experience. Achieving that level of quality takes a continuous effort to design and keep on improving the way customers interact with a company.

Customer experience and marketing strategy

Improving customer experience can help to meet many different aspects of your marketing strategy. These are some examples:

- Increase sales to existing customers.
- Improve customer satisfaction.
- Improve customer retention levels.

Set up a customer experience infrastructure

brilliant definition

Customer experience infrastructure

A customer experience infrastructure provides a framework for managing the customer relationship whenever a customer contacts your company.

Offer useful information

Gather customer data on website visits, browsing habits and requests to build a profile of their information needs. You can use that data to offer personalised services and recommendations when they visit a website. Give customer-facing staff access to the customer profiles so that they can offer a better quality response. Enhance the profiles by monitoring feedback on social networks to identify important information needs.

Provide useful information, tips and resources that customers will find valuable. Make the information easily accessible on a website and provide tools to help customers search and retrieve information. Build community facilities on the website so that customers can share information and contribute to the increased value of the site.

Improve response

Ensure that customers receive a consistent experience each time they contact your company. Give customers a choice of channels by which to communicate – telephone, email, fax or web – and provide access to the same information through each channel. Provide a single point of contact in each channel for all product or service enquiries.

brilliant tip

Monitor experience

Monitor the quality of customer experience and respond to any feedback or concerns about poor experience. Research indicates that a high proportion of customers stop dealing with a company because of a bad experience, and many relate their bad experience to other people.

Develop a response strategy

Customer responsiveness delivers excellent customer experience. Companies with strong capabilities and competences for delivering customer experience excellence are outperforming their competitors in terms of customer satisfaction. An effective customer response strategy enables a company to deliver the highest standard of customer care at a time when the customer most needs it. That level of care makes an important contribution to customer satisfaction and long-term loyalty.

Establish standards

A customer response strategy sets out procedures and quality standards for handling customer incidents and enquiries and identifies the essential infrastructure and skills. The strategy meets a wide range of objectives. It must provide the highest levels of customer support during an incident and minimise inconvenience for the customer. It will ensure that

> a customer response strategy must provide the highest levels of customer support

incidents are resolved promptly within agreed timescales and provide customers with quality response and support throughout an incident. It should also ensure that support resources are deployed effectively to maximise customer satisfaction.

Cover all channels

Customers can contact a company by telephone, email, fax or web channels. They may want to make an enquiry, order a product, place a service request, report an incident, query an invoice or make a complaint. That means that customers could be contacting many different departments and individuals.

Putting a single response strategy in place across the company ensures a consistent customer experience every time.

Invest in infrastructure

An effective customer response strategy has two main elements: the infrastructure to deliver the service and the personal skills to provide the right level of customer care.

brilliant definition

Service delivery infrastructure

The service delivery infrastructure might include communications tools to provide a rapid response to customer queries and put the service into operation, a trained support team to deliver customer service and a control centre to coordinate customer response.

Develop customer care skills

The skills requirements would include incident management skills to deal with customers who may be in stressful situations and project management skills to coordinate and implement a response. Customer-facing staff also need technical skills to deliver the service and communications skills to coordinate the elements of the response.

Improve the online experience

Simplify online purchasing. If you offer online purchasing, allow pre-registered customers to bypass a conventional shopping cart and checkout by purchasing a product with a single mouse click. The web server recognises the customer and relates their order to stored credit card and shipping information.

Keep customers on the site

The primary role of the Thank You page on an e-commerce website is to indicate that the purchase process is complete. This might be important if order processes are prone to problems: customers want to know that they have finished the process successfully, particularly if they have made an online payment. However, with more reliable order processes, the Thank You page can take a more proactive role by indicating to the customer that they can either leave the website or remain and do something else. Experience indicates that many companies assume that after completing the purchase, the customer will leave the site.

The Thank You page should be more than just a straightforward thank you. The customer has just completed a significant process – buying a product, downloading a publication, signing up for a subscription, or registering their details. When the customer is in a buying mood, that represents a great opportunity to go further.

Offer customers more options

The Thank You page offers a great opportunity for positive communication. The basic Thank You process takes very little space. There are no other distracting messages and the visitor has provided a great deal of profiling information. With such a captive audience, you can provide a number of alternatives that will benefit both parties. The page should therefore offer a number of suggested routes, which might include:

- Continue shopping.
- Return to the home page.
- Find out more about the product.
- Rate the website service.
- Check delivery status.

Suggest action

If your site is designed for lead generation and a visitor has downloaded a white paper or other publication after registering information, you now have more knowledge about their level and type of interest. You can use this knowledge to suggest routes to additional content: for example, read a case study about this industry, find out about our solutions for this industry, or contact an industry specialist. This can be a great basis for retaining customers by demonstrating the value of the content on your site.

brilliant tip

For new customers, it is important to provide careful guidance to the additional content. The more content you can expose them to and the more you can direct them to the right areas, the more likely they are to fall into a pattern of visiting that benefits you and builds long-term relationships.

Encourage impulse buys

As well as focusing on exit routes, you can also use other techniques to encourage visitors to stay on a site.

- Suggest related products at a discounted price. If an online shopper decides to buy a particular product, the closer page can offer the product at a special price if the customer buys it together with a related product.

- Suggest linked products. If a customer buys a product that has accessories, ask if they would also like to buy batteries, peripherals or other accessories. Those are items the customer may forget to purchase or might not realise are available.

- Make a limited time offer. A visitor is more likely to take advantage of a special offer if they know there's a time limit.

- Offer to group subsequent orders to reduce delivery costs. It's more efficient to pack more items in each order, so give customers an incentive to purchase more at one time. This may be important if delivery charges represent a significant proportion of a low value item.

- Offer free delivery for orders over a certain value. This may encourage customers to make additional purchases to reach the required order value.

Make the most of follow-up emails

Follow-up emails are an important part of building a relationship after the sale. There should be a series of emails advising the customer of the progress of their order:

- Confirmation of acceptance of their order.
- Advice that their product is in production.
- The product is about to be despatched.
- Delivery will be on the following date.

This keeps the customer informed in a proactive way and reduces the number of delivery enquiry calls your contact centre has to handle. You can also offer the customer a self-service facility – 'Click here to get an update on your order'. This gives the customer greater control over the process and also encourages them to continue visiting your site.

Encourage the customer to register for additional services

When a customer has completed a purchase or other transaction, offer them the opportunity to register for other relevant services:

- *Set up an account.* Although a customer may have used a one-off payment method, such as a credit card, offering them an account can encourage repeat purchase, as well as providing valuable profiling information. The account should offer the customer added value such as membership discounts or other privileges, as well as a more convenient method of ordering and payment. The account would also give the customer facilities for reviewing their purchase history, checking delivery information or making returns.

- *Offer product notifications.* This is particularly important where product changes are frequent and customers can upgrade easily. Customers agree to the notification, providing an opportunity for future communications. In return, they should be offered privileged discounts.

- *Offer support services.* Customers may need a range of services depending on the type of product. These could include installation, telephone support, routine maintenance or repair. This can provide additional revenue and strengthen the customer relationship.

- *Offer advice.* Customers may want advice and help in making the best use of their product. Direct them to a forum or other online community where they can get information, advice and support from other customers as well as experts. They can also sign up for regular newsletters that provide ongoing advice and guidance,

Improve the contact centre experience

Customer expectations are rising. While technologies like interactive voice response (IVR) systems, computer–telephony integration (CTI) and call routing have significantly enhanced the customer experience, customers continually demand further improvement. Customers expect each interaction to be at least as satisfactory as the previous one, and this puts additional strains on already stretched contact centre capabilities. Faced with the constant

> customers expect each interaction to be at least as satisfactory as the previous one

pressure to generate revenue, manage rising traffic volumes and meet ever-increasing customer service expectations, the traditional contact centre model is no longer sufficient.

Control fluctuating traffic

One of the greatest contact centre challenges is responding to fluctuating traffic. Many contact centres today struggle to meet spikes in demand or utilise idle resources when traffic drops. These challenges arise due to unpredictable events; for example, calls to internet service providers often spike sharply when there is a network problem. Similarly, a power failure or burst water main can quickly generate high call levels for a utility company.

Unfortunately, contact centre staffing levels are generally decided well in advance, making it difficult to respond to unexpected events. On the one hand, allocating contact centre agents conservatively can lead to poor service when traffic spikes. As queue times rise, customers become frustrated, and companies experience high levels of abandoned calls. On the other hand, over-scheduling agents raises costs and creates agent dissatisfaction as they sit idle or perform less valuable tasks.

Match skills with calls

Another challenge is to match different contact centre tasks with individual agents' capabilities. Some contact centre agents are expert at handling inbound calls, while others are equally comfortable handling inbound and outbound calls. Others may prefer to handle only non-voice channels such as email, web chat and instant messaging. Having agents focused on one interaction creates imbalances whenever a particular interaction channel peaks.

Balance resources

To meet those fluctuation challenges, it's important to adjust the volume and mix of available resources to meet changing conditions. At a basic level, agents could shift between activities according to their particular skill set and availability to handle multiple interaction types or manage both inbound and outbound calls. As a result, the pool of resources would instantly expand for one task and contract for another based on analysis of changing contact centre conditions. Another approach is to reallocate staff from other areas of the business or other locations. These resources could be deployed at short notice to help manage high traffic volumes or handle complicated, specialised calls.

Integrate contact channels

Many customers prefer to interact with a contact centre through non-voice channels such as email, text, chat or website. Integrating these channels ensures that customers receive a consistent customer experience across all contact centre media. This is also important for contact centre management as these alternative channels provide cost-effective options to manage traffic and outcomes by shifting the allocation of resources.

> integrating channels ensures that customers receive a consistent customer experience

Provide access to expertise

Sometimes, meeting specific customer requirements takes specialised agent skills. It's therefore essential to provide access to the skills and resources of expert staff in other locations. For example, high value banking clients can be immediately routed to a specialist in a branch office when conducting a complex transaction that may offer an upsell opportunity.

Manage complaints effectively

Make it easy for customers to complain. Set up a complaints form or public forum on your website. Provide a free telephone number for complaints. Include clear guidelines for making complaints on any product packaging or service documentation. Only a small proportion of customers with problems actually complain because they

> only a small proportion of customers with problems actually complain

feel they will not get an adequate response. Creating a transparent complaints procedure demonstrates your willingness to deal with problems.

Respond to complaints

Respond quickly to any complaints. Set standards for response times. Acknowledge the complaint immediately and let the customer know when they will receive a detailed response. Outline the escalation procedure for any complaints that you cannot resolve to the customer's satisfaction.

brilliant tip

Providing a speedy response overcomes negative perceptions of your customer service.

Explain the reason for the problem to the customer. If it is a product or service issue, tell the customer what action you will be taking to overcome the problem. Offer a refund or substitute product or service if you cannot resolve the problem immediately. Customers who feel you have resolved their complaint fairly are likely to continue to buy from you.

Monitor complaints

Monitor any complaints or negative comments on social networking sites. Respond to the comments and try to create dialogue to counter any negative perceptions. Social networking sites make it easy for dissatisfied customers to share their grievances and communicate negative comments to a very large audience.

Set up a process for managing complaints and assessing their potential impact. Companies that do not help customers to complain may have an inaccurate or overoptimistic perception of customer satisfaction. As a result they may factor incorrect repurchase behaviour into their sales and marketing forecasts. Understanding the nature and extent of complaints helps you to develop strategies to win back dissatisfied customers and increase retention levels.

Marketing plan in brief

Current situation

- Customer satisfaction is at a low level.
- Strengths of loyal existing customer base.
- Weakness of poor perception of customer experience.
- Threats of customer defection to competitors to obtain better service.
- Opportunity to improve customer satisfaction and loyalty.

Market requirements

- Customers are looking for improved standards of service in all their interactions with the company.

Objectives

- Increase sales to existing customers.
- Improve customer satisfaction.
- Improve customer retention levels.

Strategy

- Set up customer experience infrastructure.
- Develop effective response strategy.
- Improve online experience.
- Improve contact centre experience.
- Manage complaints effectively.

Financial requirements

- Investment in customer experience infrastructure.
- Budget for customer service training.

Communications

- Internal communications to raise awareness of customer service requirements.
- Customer communications to explain service improvements.

Metrics

- Changes in customer satisfaction levels.
- Changes in customer retention levels.
- Numbers of complaints.
- Website page visits.
- Website browsing times.

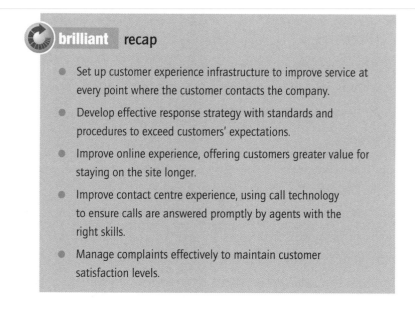

brilliant recap

- Set up customer experience infrastructure to improve service at every point where the customer contacts the company.

- Develop effective response strategy with standards and procedures to exceed customers' expectations.

- Improve online experience, offering customers greater value for staying on the site longer.

- Improve contact centre experience, using call technology to ensure calls are answered promptly by agents with the right skills.

- Manage complaints effectively to maintain customer satisfaction levels.

CHAPTER 15

Strengthen customer relationships

A key factor in the relationship between you and your customers is the value you can demonstrate. Companies that can help their customers reduce costs, improve their business performance or strengthen their competitive position can get closer to customers and build a dependent relationship. Relationship management helps to deal with low price, low quality competition, adds value to a product or service and positions your company as a partner offering a strategically important package.

Customer relationship management and marketing strategy

Strong customer relationships can help to meet many different aspects of your marketing strategy. These are some examples:

- Increase sales to existing customers.
- Build long-term revenue streams.
- Position the company in a strategic way.
- Counter competitive activity.

Build customer dependency

Products and services provide a valuable role when they support a customer's core business. The service then becomes essential to the customer's own business. For example, if a customer wanted to introduce a telemarketing programme to support its own customer relationship programmes, but didn't have the skills, facilities or resources, the supplier could provide the telesales infrastructure and integrate it with the customer's own marketing activities. The customer could then concentrate on their core business development without diverting scarce resources to handle the support activities.

Focus on customers' through-life costs

brilliant definition

Through-life cost

Through-life cost is a concept used in engineering to describe products that have a value beyond their initial purchase price. For example, a component that is higher priced may be simple to assemble, easy to maintain and have a long life. The costs of that product over a whole life are likely to be lower than those of an inferior product that may cost less initially, but prove expensive in the long run when installation, servicing and replacement costs are taken into account.

By working with the customer to identify and reduce through-life costs, you can increase account control.

Align services with the customer's life cycle

Another key concept in the customer relationship is the life cycle. By providing a range of services to supply the skills and resources customers need to complete a project and continue delivering the highest standards of service to their own customers, your company becomes involved at every stage in the life cycle of customers' products. This might take the form of helping customers reduce costs, speed up response times, improve product quality or supplement internal resources – valuable services that help to build a dependent relationship.

brilliant example

A strategic consultancy service which is aligned to its customer's future business objectives can help the customer identify the key growth paths and the skills needed to achieve those objectives. They can prepare a project plan and work with the customer's project team to meet the key requirements in a cost-effective way. They can also provide a range of services, enabling the customer to compete effectively at every stage in the life cycle.

Offer customers a package of products and services

The impact of pricing can be improved by offering customers a package of products and services that represent real value for money for their business. A manufacturer who includes installation, training and initial support in the package offers better value for money than a competitor who simply sells the product to customers and expects them to meet the costs of start-up.

By working in partnership with customers you gain an understanding of the problems and costs they incur in implementing products. They may have to acquire new skills to install the product, set up training programmes for users and support staff, and provide a high level of support during the implementation period. To help customers handle implementation more efficiently and cost effectively, you can offer services such as carrying out initial installation, providing the services of an engineer on site to improve the skills of customer support staff and provide any specialist support needed. This represents value for money because the customer does not have to recruit additional, costly staff.

Protect a customer's reputation with reliable products

A company that has a reputation for supplying high quality but expensive products can justify the cost difference by offering the customer a level of superior reliability that the customer can build into their own products. This is particularly important in the components market where companies rely on supplier quality to protect their own reputation and brand image. In some markets, for example information technology, component quality has become so important that many components are now strongly branded products in their own right.

Improve the customer's return on investment

Major expenditure can be justified by its return on investment – how well and how quickly the expenditure pays for itself in benefits to the business. For example, a major consultancy project which improves a customer's competitive edge may be expensive, but it will pay for itself in enhanced revenue, profitability and market share, providing a high return on investment. Strategically important products are more likely to provide a good return on investment than commodity products.

> strategically important products are more likely to provide a good return on investment than commodity products

Deliver strategically important products

Positioning a product or service as strategically important helps to assure customers that they are buying more than a commodity. The product or service is shown to be important to the success of the customer's business and this helps to ensure that it represents value for money.

brilliant impact

Strategically important products can help you differentiate yourself from competitors, charge higher prices and build effective relationships with customers.

Strategically important products have a number of characteristics:

- Essential to business success.
- Added value.
- Support the core business.
- Speed up business processes.
- Enable new product or market developments.
- Improve competitive performance.
- Reduce the cost of key business processes.

Differentiate products

Products and services can be differentiated on the basis of their value to the customer's business. Commodity products have little visible difference – price is similar, quality and performance equivalent, and the results similar. However, if a product is directly aimed at business needs, it can be clearly differentiated. Examples include:

- Training services to ensure customer staff get the best results from their systems.
- Project services to help customers complete essential projects faster and allow their own staff to concentrate on key business activities.

● Contract design and research services that customers can use to push their own product development programmes ahead at a faster rate and keep ahead of their competitors.

Speed up customers' business processes

Speed is an essential element in markets where the pace of change puts increasing pressure on rapid product development. A company that offers new product consultancy and provides a whole range of support services will enable faster product development. Customers can get new products to market or introduce new services more quickly without committing their own resources. Getting there quicker means that they can stay ahead of the competition and improve their response to changing market conditions – both essential to maintaining long-term turnover and profitability.

The pressure of day-to-day activities prevents many companies from concentrating on new product development or important business developments. The result is that they lag behind the competition and miss the opportunity to succeed through innovation. Suppliers can support them, either by handling the day-to-day tasks on a cost-effective basis to free the internal team or by taking on strategic development work in collaboration with the customer. Either way, it will speed up the process and provide the customer with a faster return on investment.

Help customers expand their activities

Sometimes companies are prevented from exploiting profitable new developments because they lack the skills or resources needed for success. By filling that gap in the customer's resources and demonstrating how the new development can be used to provide a strategy for growth, you can position your services as strategically important. By providing these scarce skills to supplement the customer's own resources, you can help the customer develop and introduce the new products rapidly. The customer will be able to compete effectively while continuing to concentrate on their core business.

Reduce cost of business processes

Companies also benefit from a reduction in the cost of their business processes. Using their own staff to handle everything can be expensive because certain skills may be used only occasionally. By analysing all their activities and dividing them into core and non-core activities, you can decide where support will be beneficial.

)brilliant impact

Build high levels of dependency

Just selling a product or service does not create a strong relationship with a customer. It is the added-value benefits that increase customer dependency and provide the basis for an effective, long-term relationship. The relationship can cover a wide area of collaboration from technical cooperation, shared manufacturing resources, joint ventures and development programmes to shared distribution and logistics networks. The higher the level of collaboration, the greater the dependency in the relationship.

Create a collaborative relationship

The lines between companies and their customers are increasingly blurred, with companies aiming to build a collaborative environment in which customers interact easily and participate in product development and other processes. Conferences, workshops, collaborative working and joint development projects, as well as interactive online services all help to contribute to the collegial environment. The collaborative environment is an approach to customer relationships that encourages friendly cooperation and involvement, rather than the traditional supplier/buyer relationship

Build trust and confidence

Building a collaborative atmosphere can help position your company as an influential, trusted resource. Your marketing communications work from a solid foundation of experience and expertise because you have earned the trust and respect of industry colleagues and customers. You can speak as an industry leader with a bright, concise tone, and you involve and empower your target audience. You understand their preoccupations and priorities and you help them to see how they might relate to your organisation and its activities. You demonstrate how you can help them do more.

Use a collaborative tone of voice

The language you use should create a sense of partnership and camaraderie with your audience. Your tone of voice conveys warmth, enthusiasm and a sense of fun. Your copy should speak in a conversational tone, addressing your audiences directly, and speaking on their level – not above, not below, but as a trusted and respected colleague, eye to eye. Most important, your copy should always keep your audience's interest and priorities in mind. The conversational tone conveys partnership and helps your audience understand you clearly. That means language should feel uncluttered, unfussy, easy and unpretentious. It should be personal and direct, not stuffy and institutional. It will project a familiar quality that reflects confidence and trust.

Create welcoming conferences

A collaborative atmosphere is particularly appropriate for conferences, workshops and other customer events. The ideal conference would have the feel of a reunion, characterised by involvement and a sense of being among old friends. The event would be productive, with shared information and involvement by people who are glad to be participating, and who enjoy working together in a spirit of fun and liveliness. The conference should present delegates with the latest products, identify the most important issues, provide ample networking opportunities and allow them to get involved with the industry's leading innovators in a forum that features a high level of interactive participation.

> the ideal conference would have the feel of a reunion

Set up the facilities for a community

You can extend the collaborative environment by setting up a virtual community on the internet to support electronic interaction between people with a common interest. Facilities to support the community could include newsletters, discussion groups and information. You can also use your online community facilities to allow members to join an online club and enjoy privileged services, using the membership database to offer personalised incentives and promotions.

Set up a discussion group

An online discussion group gives users the facilities for posting messages on your site. The messages should represent helpful information and may include requests for help or further information. Some sites set up facilities for feedback or product review, introducing an opportunity for objective, independent comment. The aim is to encourage other members of the community to suggest answers, provide help or contribute to the discussion of a specific issue. Discussion groups help to build credibility for the site and strengthen the relationships that are essential to the collaborative environment.

> **brilliant** tip
>
> In the early stages of a community site, it's important to have good content, so that visitors can get a feel for how they are expected to act. Set up some initial threads and encourage 'friendly' members to start discussions.

Support collaborative working

Many companies are finding that, to compete in the increasingly global marketplace, they need to involve specialists outside their own organisation in the product development process. By collaborating and creating efficient joint teams, they can tackle key challenges in the product development process, reduce time to market, improve the success rate of new products, and grow market share and revenues. By using collaborative technologies, they can share accurate, up-to-date digital product information across different companies as well as across different functions such as design, engineering, manufacturing, marketing sales, and purchasing. They can include suppliers, partners, and customers in an 'extended enterprise' with the aim of creating higher quality products, increasing innovation, and reducing development lead times.

Your virtual community could be used to support this type of collaborative working. Customers and other members answer each others' technical questions and help each other out, publicly, on the community website. The site could also provide shared access to design and technical tools that customers can use on their own projects. As part of the collaborative environment, you could set up virtual project rooms where teams from different organisations can collaborate on a project using the site database and pull in third-party resources as they need them. Secure communication systems and sophisticated collaboration tools mean that dispersed team members can work together effectively in a 'virtual enterprise'.

Marketing plan in brief

Current situation

- Customer relationships are weak and complaints are increasing.
- Strengths of diverse customer base.
- Weakness of poor customer service performance.
- Threat of customers switching suppliers.
- Opportunity to build dependent relationships.

Market requirements

- Products and a level of service to help customers improve their own business performance.

Objectives

- Increase sales to existing customers.
- Build long-term revenue streams.
- Position the company in a strategic way.
- Counter competitive activity.

Strategy

- Build customer dependency.
- Deliver strategically important products.
- Create a collaborative relationship.

Financial requirements

- Invest in product development to deliver customer-focused products.

Communications

- Customer communications to build frequency of contact and improve collaboration.

Metrics

- Increase in long-term sales, revenue or profit.
- Increase in sales to existing customers.
- Increase in customer retention levels.

brilliant recap

- Build customer dependency by providing products and services that help them improve their own business processes.
- Deliver strategically important products that enable customers to build a competitive advantage.
- Create a collaborative environment to build stronger and more valuable relationships with customers.

Conclusion: Keep tuned to the market

Marketing planning is a dynamic process because market conditions are changing so rapidly. Just a few years ago, Facebook, Twitter and other social media were seen as something for consumers. Now they're mainstream business media.

Cloud computing is a term you might have heard about if you walked past the IT department. You'll be hearing a lot more about it in marketing because it's set to give you some powerful new tools. What would you give for instant IT resources when you're running a major launch or managing campaign response? Wouldn't it be great to have access to vast amounts of market data so that you can create personalised marketing campaigns? Cloud computing will make that possible without a massive investment in new IT systems.

Using technology will become a more important part of the marketing role in the same way as salesforce.com supports sales management. It's not technology for its own sake, it's there to help you deal with the increasing pace of change, the growing number of competitors from emerging markets and the demand for more and more information.

So, more than ever, you need to monitor what your customers are looking for and what they think about you and your competitors. The internet and the exchange of information on social media have made business much more transparent. Customers expect and demand more from suppliers and, if you fail to meet expectations, a lot of people will soon know about it.

The more you understand about your customers and the market, the more effectively you can respond with new products, new campaigns, new channels to market and new sales initiatives. Technology gives you the tools to keep tuned to the market. Couple that with mastery of the techniques in this book and you'll be equipped to deliver brilliant marketing results.

Index